A GANNETT COMPANY

Lifeline

BIOGRAPHIES

LADY GAGA

Pop's Glam Queen

by Matt Doeden

Twenty-First Century Books · Minneapolis

Twenty-First Century Books
A division of Lerner Publishing Group, Inc.
241 First Avenue North
Minneapolis, MN 55401 U.S.A.

Website address: www.lernerbooks.com

Library of Congress Cataloging-in-Publication Data

Doeden, Matt.
Lady Gaga : pop's glam queen / by Matt Doeden.
p. cm. – (USA Today lifeline biographies)
Includes bibliographical references and index.
ISBN 978-0-7613-8153-2 (lib. bdg. : alk. paper)
1. Lady Gaga—Juvenile literature. 2. Singers—United States—Biography—Juvenile literature. I. Title.
ML3930.L13D64 2012
782.42164092—dc23 [B] 2011021294

Manufactured in the United States of America
1 – PP – 12/31/11

USA TODAY
A GANNETT COMPANY
Lifeline BIOGRAPHIES

Smooch: Lady Gaga gives Kermit the Frog a kiss during her arrival at the 2009 MTV Video Music Awards at Radio City Music Hall in New York City.

A Night to Remember

On September 13, 2009, music stars from around the world gathered at Radio City Music Hall in New York City for one of the biggest nights in the music industry—the MTV Video Music Awards (VMA). It was a night for the stars of the industry to shine, and few shone brighter than Stefani Joanne Angelina Germanotta, better known to the world as Lady Gaga.

In the previous year, Lady Gaga had risen from obscurity to the top of the music industry, riding the strength of her pop hits "Poker Face" and "Just Dance." She was known as much for her wild sense of style as for her catchy tunes. Fans and media wondered what kind of outfit she would show off for the VMA, and she didn't disappoint. In fact, she didn't wear one outfit. She wore five different outfits that evening! Escorted to the awards by famous Muppet Kermit the Frog (whom she left in the limousine that drove her to the awards), Lady Gaga arrived in a black lace dress, a feathered neck brace, and a golden eye patch. Photographers flocked to her, eager to get a snapshot of pop's hottest new artist.

That night Lady Gaga was nominated for nine awards and also performed to an enthusiastic audience. Once inside, she had little time to waste—she was scheduled to perform almost right away. She hurried off to a dressing room and her first change of clothes. She slipped into a two-piece lacy white outfit with thigh-high boots and an elaborate mask. Lady Gaga appeared before a packed house to perform her latest hit, "Paparazzi." (The term *paparazzi* refers to photographers who follow celebrities in the hopes of getting revealing photos of them.)

Lady Gaga is no ordinary performer, though, and singing and dancing weren't enough for her that evening. She wanted to make sure everyone would be talking about her the next day. And she and her dancers had just the routine to make that happen. Cheered on by the audience, Lady Gaga and her male and female dancers—all dressed in tight-fitting white outfits—sang and pranced onstage. Then Lady Gaga strode to her white piano and knocked out a few eerie chords before returning to the center of the stage. There, fake blood suddenly began to gush out of her chest, running down her legs and staining her pure white outfit. Her dancers surrounded her as she cried out in mock terror and agony. They lifted her off the stage, one of her arms hanging from a cord suspended from the ceiling. Her head dangled to one side, as the final act of her staged suicide by hanging. The audience rose

to their feet in thunderous ovation. They loved the way this star had made a gory and powerful statement about the price of fame.

The night only got more exciting for the twenty-three-year-old star. She won the VMA for Best New Artist and accepted it onstage, dressed in a see-through red lace minidress. She said little onstage,

Covered in red: Lady Gaga *(left)* staged a hanging during her performance of "Paparazzi" at the MTV Video Music Awards on September 13, 2009. Lady Gaga, covered in red lace *(right)*, accepts the 2009 MTV Video Music Award for Best New Artist.

December 29, 2009

Lady Gaga: Playing the 'Fame' game

From the Pages of USA TODAY

The 23-year-old singer/songwriter became 2009's hottest new diva by drawing on previous pop movements from glam rock (Queen's "Radio Ga Ga" is the source of her nom de fame) to Madonna. Like that earlier paragon of bleached-blond ambition, the artist born Stefani Joanne Angelina Germanotta is an Italian-American gal who did time both in Catholic school and on the downtown New York club scene. Gaga's flamboyant live performances and button-pushing professions of bisexuality earned as much attention as her hit album *The Fame* and smash single "Poker Face," which collectively earned her five Grammy nominations.

—Elysa Gardner, Brian Mansfield, Steve Jones, Jerry Shriver

removing her red lace face veil and crown long enough to thank "God and her gays." It was a nod to Lady Gaga's large following in the gay community, which she credits with much of her success.

Before the memorable night was over, Lady Gaga had changed costumes multiple times and collected two more awards. "The VMA performance was the big, total platter offering of Lady Gaga to the industry audience who might not have known her then," said MTV's Liz Gateley.

Lady Gaga had come to the award show as a pop star. She left it as a cultural icon.

Young Gaga: Stefani Joanne Angelina Germanotta, later known as Lady Gaga, is pictured here as a young girl playing with a puppy.

Little Gaga

Stefani Joanne Angelina Germanotta was born March 28, 1986, in New York City. Her parents, Joseph and Cynthia, were Internet businesspeople and made a comfortable living off the growing technology. She was the family's first child, joined six years later by a little sister, Natali.

The family lived on New York's Upper West Side. It was a good neighborhood, and Stefani had access to all the art and culture of the

New York City: Stefani and her family moved to the Pythian building *(above)*, on New York's Upper West Side in 1993.

city. By the 1990s, the Internet was taking off and Joseph had a very successful business setting up Internet access for hotels and other businesses. Cynthia worked in telecommunications. The couple was by no means wealthy, but they were comfortable and able to provide well for their two girls.

Born to Entertain

Stefani was an entertainer from the beginning. She learned to play the piano at the age of four. Although she hated the lessons, she always had a strong desire to perform. "I was in the [play] *Three Billy Goats Gruff* when I was in kindergarten," she recalled. "I was the big billy goat—I decided to make my horns out of tinfoil and a hanger."

Starting at the age of eleven, Stefani attended a private, all-girls Catholic school called Convent of the Sacred Heart. It was an expensive

and very exclusive school whose alumni (previous students) included the famous Hilton sisters, Paris and Nicky. While the school had its share of the ultrarich, it wasn't just for the wealthy. "Sacred Heart may have been prestigious, but there were lots of different kinds of girls," Stefani later said. "Some had extreme wealth, others were on welfare and scholarship, and some were in the middle, which was my family. All our money went into education and the house."

Stefani was one of few students at Sacred Heart who had an after-school job. She worked as a waitress. She recalls that earning—and spending—her own money was an exciting and rewarding experience.

Stefani claims that she never fit in with the other students and that she felt like a freak while in school. She described herself as artsy and unable to fit in with the crowd. She remembers that some students called her the Germ, a play on her last name. "For a little while, I thought girls were just jealous [of me]," she later explained. "But I think I genuinely used to rub people in the wrong way. I'd talk about things and do things that were very . . . over the top, and very vain."

While Lady Gaga insists that she was an outcast in school, many of her classmates paint a different picture. They say that she was well liked and fit in with the others. "She was always popular," said one classmate. "I don't remember her experiencing any social problems or awkwardness."

One thing everyone agrees on is that Stefani loved to perform. She began acting classes at the age of eleven and later starred in school productions such as the musicals *Guys and Dolls* and *A Funny Thing Happened on the Way to the Forum*. She wrote her first song, titled "To Love Again," at the age of thirteen. "Stefani was always part of school plays and musicals," said another classmate. "She liked boys a lot, but

her singing and her passion for the arts were number one for her. . . . It was plain to see that she was going to be a star."

Building for the Future

Stefani loved acting, but music soon became her main passion and her goal in life. By the age of fifteen, she was a regular at open-mike nights at local clubs such as the Bitter End. (On open-mike nights, anyone can take the stage to perform for the audience.) She would play piano and sing, with her mother watching from the audience. Meanwhile, she also started her own rock cover band. They performed popular songs from other artists, such as Pink Floyd and the Beatles. And she continued to compose original music as well. At her sixteenth birthday party, she gave all her friends a copy of her demo, a disk that featured her singing love songs she'd written herself.

Classmates: Sixteen-year-old Stefani *(left)* takes a picture with her classmates at a Christmas dance. Stefani went to Convent of the Sacred Heart Catholic school in New York.

IN FOCUS

Musical Influence: Britney Spears

As a teen, Stefani was a big fan of pop star Britney Spears. When Stefani was in high school, she went to see Spears at a public appearance. Stefani was so excited by the chance just to be near the star that she was in tears.

Britney Jean Spears was born December 2, 1981. As a child, she dabbled in acting before signing with Jive Records in 1997. Spears released her first album, . . . *Baby One More Time*, in 1997 and quickly became a teen sensation. Her upbeat dance songs, provocative outfits and choreography, and natural beauty made her a pop culture icon and the subject of nearly constant gossip and rumor. The album sold more than 10 million copies within a year. Spears struck gold again with her follow-up album, 2000's *Oops, I Did It Again*. Spears released five more albums over the next eleven years and has maintained a loyal fan base.

Pop star: Britney Spears performs in 1999. As a teenager, Stefani was a big fan of the singer.

Stefani's parents encouraged their eldest daughter's artistic side. They drove her to performances, took her into adult nightclubs where she could perform, and always supported her passion. "My parents were very supportive of anything creative I wanted to do, whether it was playing piano or being in plays and taking . . . acting classes," she said. "They liked that I was a motivated young person."

While Stefani got good grades in school, she also had a rebellious streak. She got a fake ID so she could get into nightclubs on her own. At

Lady Gaga credits her mother's sense of style with sparking her own love of clothing. "[My mother] always looked so much more pristine [neat and tidy] than all the other mothers," she said. "I have a lot of her in me. I went through periods where I was very sexy, then I became a hippie girl with ripped jeans, and then went into a leopard-tights-and-leotards phase, which I'm still in. Fashion saved my life! When I was young, I was laughed at in school because I dressed dramatically."

one point, she dated a man ten years older than she was. She got a tattoo. She wore low-cut shirts to school, which earned her a scolding from her teachers. She wanted to be different, to stand out from the crowd. And it was this desire not to conform, she said, that gave her troubles in high school. She felt that some of the other girls resented her style and sense of individualism.

Stefani was eager to leave high school behind her, and at the age of seventeen, she got her wish. She applied for and gained early admittance into New York University's (NYU) Tisch School

Role models: Lady Gaga's parents, Cynthia and Joseph Germanotta, pose for a picture in 2010. Gaga said her mother has always had a sense of fashion.

USA TODAY Snapshots®

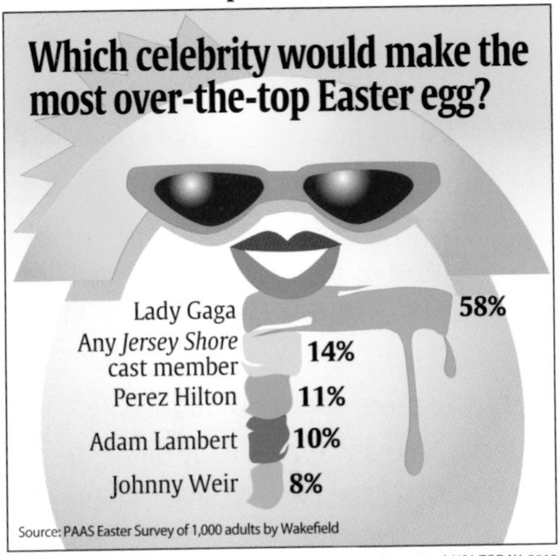

Which celebrity would make the most over-the-top Easter egg?

Celebrity	Percent
Lady Gaga	58%
Any *Jersey Shore* cast member	14%
Perez Hilton	11%
Adam Lambert	10%
Johnny Weir	8%

Source: PAAS Easter Survey of 1,000 adults by Wakefield

By Michelle Healy and Sam Ward, USA TODAY, 2010

of the Arts. Tisch is a prestigious school best known for it drama program. Its list of alumni reads like a who's who of Hollywood, from Angelina Jolie and Anne Hathaway to film directors M. Night Shyamalan and Oliver Stone.

Stefani moved into a dorm and began attending classes. But her excitement was soon tempered. She found that the classes didn't really challenge her creatively. She felt that other students lagged behind her and that she wasn't learning much. "Once you learn how to think about art, you can teach yourself," she said.

Rocker Girl

Despite her growing frustration, Stefani stuck it out at NYU for a little more than a year. Her classmates remember her as a very focused student, but her true passion was outside of the classroom. She started the Stefani Germanotta Band with some fellow NYU students. The band was a four piece, featuring Stefani on vocals and keyboards, Eli Silverman on guitar, Calvin Pia on bass, and Alex Beckman on drums. The band had a straight melodic rock sound, which was featured on their only album release, 2006's *Red and Blue*, which they sold at their shows. One student who tried out for the band described the band's sound as piano rock, like a female version of popular singer Billy Joel.

"It was all very normal, very singer-songwritery," another friend said of the music. "It was just the Stefani Germanotta Band. She'd have

her piano standing up. The band, to be honest, they weren't that great. I always thought she was talented. I'm sure she realized, 'I gotta do something unique.'"]

The band performed at local clubs and attracted a small amount of attention. Stefani later recalled a show in front of talent scouts from Columbia Records. She said they were confused about the band's sound. "We get [Stefani's voice]," one of them said, "but we don't get the music." The problem was a matter of identity. Stefani was trying hard to be a rocker, but it was a style that didn't suit her vocal abilities or personality very well.

Meanwhile, Stefani was growing more and more dissatisfied with her education. She wanted to leave NYU and focus solely on her music. She told her parents about her plan. Stefani's father, ever supportive, made a deal with his eighteen-year-old daughter. He would pay her rent for one year while she tried to make her name in music. If, after that time, she hadn't made it, she would reenroll at NYU. The clock was ticking, and a new stage of Stefani's life was about to begin.

Family support: Lady Gaga *(right)* and her sister, Natali, and their father, Joseph, celebrate Gaga's 2011 Council of Fashion Designers of America Fashion Icon Award. Joseph paid Lady Gaga's rent for a year while she tried to make it in the music industry.

www.usatoday.com

USA TODAY
A GANNETT COMPANY

CHAPTER TWO

Rockin': Stefani sings and plays the piano with the Stefani Germanotta Band at a rock club in New York City in 2005.

Paying Her Dues

March 2005 was a time of change for Stefani. Just before her nineteenth birthday, she moved into an inexpensive apartment on Manhattan's Lower East Side. This former immigrant, working-class neighborhood was becoming very hip and trendy in the early 2000s. Funky music clubs and other venues for the performing arts made the neighborhood attractive to young Stefani. She wanted to look the part of a rocker,

Powerful: After Stefani moved out of her parents' home, she lived in this apartment building on the Lower East Side of New York City. Her apartment had only a few pieces of furniture.

so she straightened her naturally curly dark hair and dyed it jet black. By this time, the Stefani Germanotta Band had recorded a demo and was a regular feature on the local club scene. Stefani was dating one of her fellow bandmates. It was only a matter of time, Stefani believed, before her talent would be discovered.

Self-Destructive Behavior

Being on her own, away from her parents and from school, gave Stefani a sense of freedom. She had long felt trapped by the strict atmosphere of Sacred Heart and was ready to cut loose. Living on her own brought out a wild side in Stefani. Many nights, she would perform with her band in clubs before small audiences, then party and drink heavily. She also began to experiment with illegal drugs.

In the fall of 2005, she took a job as a burlesque singer. Burlesque is a type of entertainment that combines singing with an elaborate stage show. Female burlesque performers often wear very skimpy outfits and dance in a very sexually suggestive manner. Stefani's parents had been steadfastly supportive of their daughter, but this was more than they were prepared to accept. Her father came to one of her shows and found that he couldn't even look at his daughter. A rift grew between Stefani and her parents.

The family problems weren't all about the burlesque show. Stefani's experimentation with illegal drugs had grown into a serious problem. Soon she was addicted to cocaine. She would sit alone in her apartment, snorting cocaine and listening to music. Even her friends, many of whom used drugs themselves, saw that Stefani was in trouble. Finally, Joseph came to speak to his daughter. "He looked at me one day and said, 'You're [screwing] up, kid,'" Stefani recalled. She has a deep respect for her father and wanted his approval. It was a wake-up call, and she resolved to control her unhealthy habits. She later wrote a song, "Beautiful, Dirty, Rich," whose lyrics touch on her experiences with drug addiction during this time.

Discovered

To learn more about the music industry, Stefani took an internship (a short-term, entry-level job that offers exposure to a profession) for music producer Irwin Robinson. She had little responsibility other than answering phones and getting coffee for Robinson. All the same, it allowed her to see the business side of the industry and gave her a clearer picture of how to succeed.

Scout: Musician and talent scout Wendy Starland, pictured here in 2007, met Stefani, then nineteen, and brought her to record producer Rob Fusari.

At about this time, nineteen-year-old Stefani met Wendy Starland, a singer, songwriter, and talent scout for record producer Rob Fusari. Fusari was well known in the industry. He had produced hits for artists such as Whitney Houston, Destiny's Child, and Will Smith. He had asked Starland to find him a young female vocalist. Starland later

Lady Gaga continues to praise Wendy Starland for discovering her. "Wendy Starland changed my life," Lady Gaga wrote. "Wendy was the angel that fulfilled my promise to my father one year before, on my 19th birthday. Without Wendy's remarkable ears, hearing through my rough-around-the-edges college band . . . I may never have become Lady Gaga."

recalled, "'Rob said to me, 'I want you to find a girl under 25 who could be the lead singer of the Strokes [a popular rock band fronted by a female singer].' I looked high and low."

One night Starland and Stefani were both to perform at a New York club called the Cutting Room. Stefani knew who Starland was and introduced herself. The two started talking. Starland later recalled their meeting. She said, "[Stefani] was wearing jeans and a T-shirt. Her band was awful, in my opinion. They were college boys, and she seemed to be modeling herself after Fiona Apple [an alternative rock and jazz singer-songwriter]. Yet when Stefani started singing, I was hooked. She had incredible confidence, she carried the crowd even though, in my opinion, the songs were bad. I grabbed hold of her [after her show] and said I was going to change her life forever."

Starland knew she'd found her star. She immediately called Fusari to set up a meeting between the two. Fusari went online to download some of Stefani's music, and he was not impressed. He told Starland that he wasn't even sure it was worth meeting Stefani. But Starland insisted that he needed to hear her live before making any decisions. Fusari finally agreed, and they set up a meeting. When Stefani walked into the room, Fusari's hopes didn't get any brighter. "She was a little

overweight," he recalled. "She looked like something out of [the 1990 crime movie] *Good Fellas*. . . . She had on leggings and some strange cut-up shirt, a hat that looked like it was out of Prince's *Purple Rain*—I remember thinking, 'That could be her. But I hope it's not.'"

Stefani's look may not have impressed Fusari, but her voice did. According to Fusari, Stefani sang for only about ten seconds before he knew that he wanted to sign her to a management contract—immediately. The two began discussing the terms of a deal. To Fusari's surprise, Stefani had a great deal more business sense than most young talent just looking for a break. She insisted on—and got—an 80-20 deal. That meant that 80 percent of whatever she earned would go straight to Stefani (and to her father). Fusari would get the remaining 20 percent. Few struggling artists would have the confidence to demand this type of deal, which gives so much money to the artist, much less get it. Fusari later admitted that Stefani's hardcore negotiation almost

Management: Lady Gaga stands with record producer Rob Fusari at his New Jersey recording studio in 2006.

caused him to walk away from the deal altogether.

USA TODAY Snapshots®

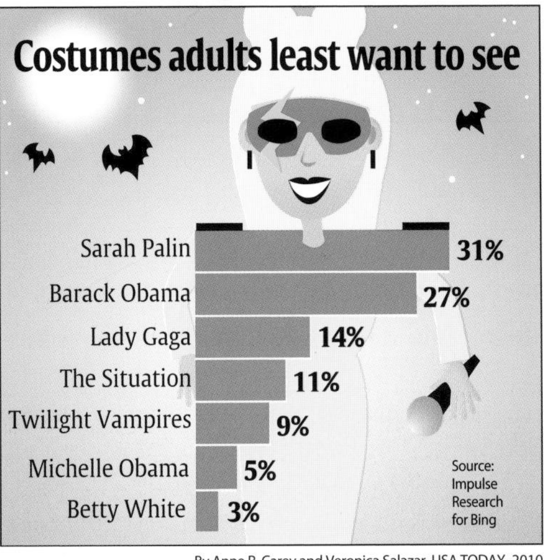

By Anne R. Carey and Veronica Salazar, USA TODAY, 2010

New Style, New Look, New Name

At this time, Stefani was an unfinished product. Fusari didn't buy into her rocker girl persona. It wasn't marketable, and rock music didn't properly suit her musical talent. It was time for a complete makeover—look, sound, style, everything. The only thing he wanted to keep was the voice.

Stefani left her band, breaking up with her boyfriend in the process. She and Fusari headed into the studio to begin crafting a new sound—more pop, less rock. They didn't always agree. Stefani wanted to move toward a singer-songwriter style that showcased her individuality and style. Fusari, on the other hand, was looking for a dance sound, a little more polished and European-sounding. In the end, Fusari got his way, and Stefani moved toward a more beat-driven pop style.

Stefani's sound wasn't the only thing that changed. It was also time to figure out a new look. Fusari wanted Stefani to lose some weight. Over the next few months, she dieted, worked out, and dropped 15 pounds (7 kilograms). They wanted to marry her look to her sound. Stefani knew that she was not a classic beauty. Fusari wanted her to play off of an exotic feel, both in her look and her sound. Stefani ran with the idea, creating an over-the-top style all her own, complete with skimpy outfits, wild hairdos, and futuristic-looking clothing. She was eager to challenge people's ideas of what fashion was all about.

Musical Influence: Freddie Mercury

Freddie Mercury was one of Lady Gaga's musical heroes. She admired his flamboyant style and amazing vocal talent. Mercury was the stage name for Farrokh Bulsara, a British musician born on September 5, 1946. Mercury was best known for fronting the legendary band Queen, with whom he recorded hits such as "Bohemian Rhapsody," "Crazy Little Thing Called Love," and "We Are the Champions." Mercury was known for his amazing voice, which covered a range of four octaves (an octave is the musical space between eight consecutive notes. Few singers can perform in more than two or three octaves). Many considered him a musical genius, and he drew influences from all sorts of musical styles, from heavy metal to gospel to disco. A 2009 poll by the British magazine *Classic Rock* named him the greatest rock singer of all time.

Mercury was diagnosed with acquired immunodeficiency syndrome (AIDS) in 1987. Although he was out about his homosexuality, he hid his illness from the public until just before his death in 1991. He was forty-five years old.

British rock: Queen performs in 1977. Lady Gaga got her name from the band's song "Radio Ga Ga." Freddie Mercury *(center)* was one of Lady Gaga's many musical influences.

Slowly, a new artist was emerging. She was a blend of ideas—something that was Stefani at the core but was also something very new and different. All that remained was to choose a stage name. Stefani and Fusari went back and forth. They finally drew their inspiration from a 1984 song called "Radio Ga Ga" by the British rock band Queen. And so Lady Gaga was born.

Duo: Lady Gaga *(right)* did shows around New York with burlesque dancer Lady Starlight *(left)*, pictured here in 2007.

Becoming Lady Gaga

Lady Gaga—still just nineteen years old—had a new look, a new sound, and a new name. But that didn't mean she was a sudden success. It was time for her to build a reputation and search for a record label. She began doing shows with a burlesque dancer who went by the name Lady Starlight. The two combined music with elements of

burlesque, performing at clubs around New York. Starlight and Gaga were quite the pair. They looked so similar that many people had a hard time telling them apart. Working with a skilled dancer like Starlight helped Gaga craft the entertainment persona she would become.

Lady Gaga spent almost all of her free time writing and recording. She had a brief fling with Tommy Kafafian, a musician who worked in the studio with Fusari. "It wasn't like we were in love at all," Kafafian said of their relationship. "It was more like, we'd hang out hours and hours and days on end in the studio, and I'd drive her home."

The collaboration between Lady Gaga and Kafafian was fruitful. Their studio time resulted in a handful of recordings that Fusari could shop to record labels. Most notable among these early songs were "Beautiful, Dirty, Rich," "Paparazzi," and "Brown Eyes."

Fusari had also developed romantic feelings for his new star. When he learned of her relationship with Kafafian, he immediately fired him. The couple soon split, however, and Lady Gaga was crushed by the breakup. Furthermore, she was confused about how to handle Fusari. She didn't have romantic feelings for him, and she knew he was engaged. But once his feelings for her became clear, Lady Gaga worried that he might cut her loose if she didn't get involved with him. In the end, her fear won out, and she began a relationship with him, a decision she later regretted deeply.

Island Def Jam

All this time, Lady Gaga continued to hone her live act. She performed as often as she could, sometimes with Lady Starlight, sometimes billed solo as Lady Gaga, and sometimes as the Plastic Gaga Band. "I played every club in New York City," she said. "I bombed in every club, and then I killed it in every club. I did it the way you are supposed to: You go and you play and pay your dues and work hard."

Meanwhile, her music was gaining a small measure of attention online. She'd posted singles to her MySpace page, as well as to other

IN FOCUS

Why Plastic?

For a short time, Lady Gaga performed with a band that she called the Plastic Gaga Band—a band made up of whomever she could get to take the stage with her on a particular night. The name was a nod to the Plastic Ono Band, formed by former Beatle John Lennon and his wife Yoko Ono in 1969. The Plastic Ono Band had no set lineup—famous and not-so-famous musicians came and went as they pleased. Lennon and Ono described their band as made up of whomever they were working with at the moment. In 2009 the couple's son, Sean Lennon, joined with his mother to revive the Plastic Ono Band. In October of that year, Lady Gaga was one of the many special guests to perform with the band at a concert in Los Angeles, California.

Collaboration: Lady Gaga *(left)* performs with Yoko Ono and the Plastic Ono Band in 2010.

online music sites, and was getting positive response. This made her lack of success in finding a record label all the more frustrating.

Finally, in late 2006, Lady Gaga caught a break. She got a meeting for an audition with a label called Island Def Jam. The exact details of this meeting aren't entirely clear—different people have shared very different accounts of what happened there. But according to many, it played out this way: Lady Gaga sang and played piano for the label's executives. At one point during her audition, she saw one of the executives get up and leave the room. That was not a good sign, she thought.

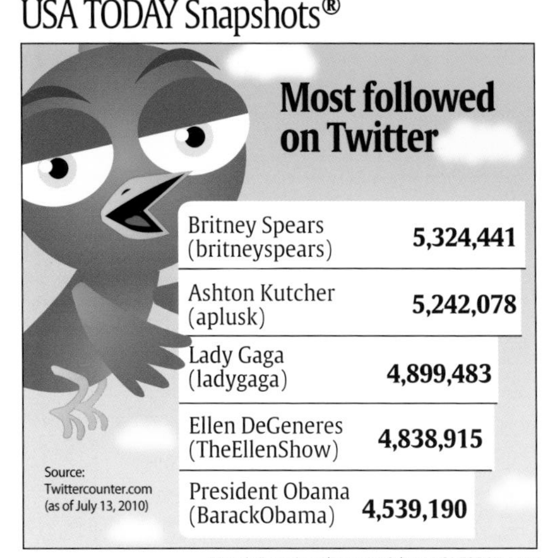

USA TODAY Snapshots®
Most followed on Twitter
Britney Spears (britneyspears) 5,324,441
Ashton Kutcher (aplusk) 5,242,078
Lady Gaga (ladygaga) 4,899,483
Ellen DeGeneres (TheEllenShow) 4,838,915
President Obama (BarackObama) 4,539,190
Source: Twittercounter.com (as of July 13, 2010)

By Michelle Healy and Veronica Salazar, USA TODAY, 2010

But she couldn't have been more wrong. The executive wasn't leaving because the performance was bad. He was getting the wheels in motion to sign the nineteen-year-old to his record label.

When Lady Gaga had finished her audition, she looked up to see the head of the label, Antonio "L. A." Reid, standing in the doorway. He told her not to leave the building until she had signed a contract. According to Lady Gaga, the contract was for $850,000—a jaw-dropping amount for almost any artist, least of all a complete unknown. Some have disputed her claim, saying that the figure isn't realistic. However, others in the know have said that, indeed, was the deal. Of that money, Fusari would get his 20 percent cut. Stefani had also hired a new manager, Laurent Besencon, who took another 20 percent. Starland also got a cut, as did a production company Stefani has formed with her father and Fusari. So while the contract might have sounded huge, in truth, Lady Gaga only got a fraction of that money.

Regardless, Lady Gaga was finally signed to a major record label. She started working with new producers, including industry legend Tom Lord-Alge and Nadir Khayat, who goes by the name RedOne. In particular, Lady Gaga and RedOne really clicked, beginning a partnership that would eventually elevate both to the peak of their professions. They worked together to take Lady Gaga's music to the next level and to develop her unique sound.

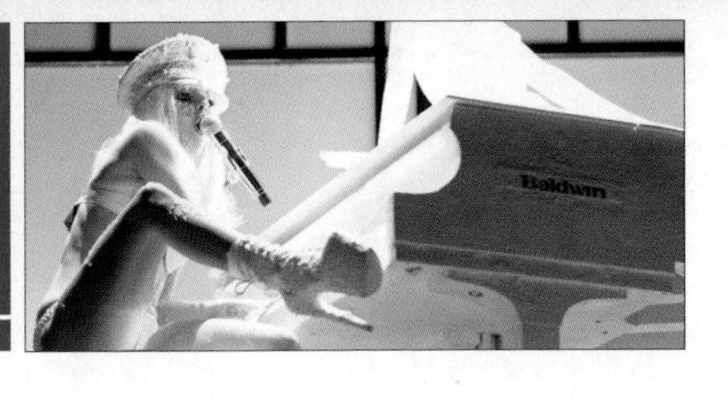

January 25, 2011

RedOne achieves monster fame

From the Pages of USA TODAY

He's a red-hot producer with a blue-chip vision. RedOne, pop's master of grabby melodies, buoyant beats and colorful sonic kinks, imagines building a musical portfolio as respected as those of [record producer] heroes George Martin and Quincy Jones. After years of struggle and setbacks, the Moroccan native has established a record of creative and commercial triumphs amid the music industry's vagaries and volatility.

After all, RedOne was the linchpin that turned disco freak show Lady Gaga into a mainstream goldmine. Last year, they shared the dance-recording Grammy for "Poker Face." This year, he's nominated (with Gaga and other participants) for best album, *The Fame Monster*. He's also up for producer of the year for *Monster* and Gaga singles "Alejandro" and "Bad Romance," plus Enrique Iglesias' "I Like It," Usher's "More," Mary J. Blige's "Whole Lotta Love" and the all-star "We Are the World: 25 for Haiti."

"I don't want to copy whatever is already out there," he says, insisting there is no single RedOne Sound. "A lot of people try to label you. I'm not a [synthesizer] guy, and I'm not a beat-maker. I'm a guitar player, a musician, a songwriter. Melody is the universal language. Give people melody, emotion and a simple lyric they can sing anywhere in the world."

RedOne's production philosophy has little to do with studio gadgetry or buckets of gloss. "No matter how hot a track is, it has to be a great song first," he says. "I've heard a lot of covers of 'Poker Face' and 'Bad Romance' on just a guitar, and it sounds good."

In the studio, his board-side manner is both pushy and Zen. "I get the best out of the artist, but not by being negative," RedOne says. "Be fun, make the artist feel good. I will tell them, 'It's good, but . . . it's not good enough.' I never say it's bad. Don't kill the beautiful vibe."

RedOne credits supportive relatives for that vital lesson. Born Nadir Khayat in the northern Moroccan city of Tetouan, he was the youngest of nine children in a close-knit family of avid musicians. He was exposed to a wide spectrum of music in a multicultural region that embraced African, European, Middle Eastern and Western sounds. He started as a singer/guitarist and subconsciously functioned as a producer.

Gradually, RedOne made inroads as a producer in Sweden, stamping hits for the A-Teens and Darin.

"There's a lot of talent in Sweden, but I wanted to go global," he says. "Every summer when I went to Morocco, they weren't hearing my songs. It killed me."

In 2006, RedOne did go global with his "Bamboo" hit, chosen as the World Cup's official melody. He produced a mash-up of the tune with Shakira's "Hips Don't Lie," featuring Wyclef Jean, that was performed at the Cup final to an estimated 260 million viewers. For RedOne, newly married and relocated in New York, it opened fewer doors than expected.

"It's because soccer is the biggest sport by far everywhere in the world, except in America," he says. "I had to struggle more. My wife and I had an air mattress in our apartment, that's it. I lost all the money I had saved. There was no work. I never thought of giving up this dream until I got married, because here is another person to take care of."

On New Year's Eve 2006, RedOne's resolve cracked while he and wife Laila were watching Jennifer Lopez in the biopic [film] *Selena*. "She got killed, and I broke down," he says. "In the new year, you think back, how was my year? I had given my life to this, and I felt like nobody was giving me a chance. I told Laila, 'I can't do this anymore.' She said, 'We're not dying, we're not in a war, we're blessed. If worse comes to worst, we'll go back to Sweden.' We borrowed money from her sister and decided to stay three more months."

Lopez proved pivotal in RedOne's U.S. launch. Within a week, Epic summoned RedOne for a Lopez remix. Karma, he thought. The label decided against releasing the track but paired RedOne with newly signed pop singer Kat DeLuna to co-write and produce *Whine Up*.

After working for years with unknowns, RedOne was determined to take on only signed artists. Yet he reluctantly agreed to meet a quirky underground singer who'd been dropped by Def Jam. Lady Gaga.

"There she was, the big glasses, the clothing, the attitude," he recalls. "She was interesting, special. That got me right away. She knew music, and I asked her to go to the studio that day. We did the first song, 'Boys Boys Boys,' and I felt like a new sound was born."

Singer/rapper Akon, an early Gaga enthusiast and RedOne booster, was impressed, but others dismissed her club-based sound as unmarketable.

"It got a lot of resistance" from industry elites, says RedOne, who co-wrote and produced five tracks on Gaga's 2008 debut, *The Fame*, and four on 2009 follow-up *The Fame Monster*.

"From day one, I knew RedOne was going to be one of the most prolific producers of our generation," says Akon.

Billboard named RedOne among 2010's top 10 producers. In 2009, he ranked first among producers and second among songwriters (behind Lady Gaga).

—Edna Gundersen

Lady Gaga later described the relationship. "RedOne is like the heart and soul of my universe," she said. "I met him and he completely, one hundred and fifty thousand percent wrapped his arms around my talent, and it was like we needed to work together. . . . His influence on me has been tremendous. I really couldn't have done it without him."

Heart and soul: Record producer RedOne attends an awards ceremony in 2011. He helped develop Lady Gaga's sound.

Dark Days

At the time, it may have seemed that Lady Gaga was well on her way to stardom. But that wasn't quite true. Her early studio work with Island Def Jam apparently didn't impress L. A. Reid. For reasons that still aren't entirely clear, Island Def Jam dropped Lady Gaga in March 2007, just three months after her contract was signed. Just like that, she was once again a performer without an album and without a record label.

Stefani was devastated. "It was the worst day of my life," she said of the day she was told of the label's decision. Just when her career had seemed to be finally taking off, she'd suffered a major setback.

There was good news, however. Normally an artist only gets paid if he or she actually releases an album under a label. But Lady Gaga's advisers found a loophole in the Island Def Jam contract, forcing the label to pay her.

Meanwhile, her personal life was hitting a rocky patch as well. Her relationship with Fusari was falling apart. She began seeing Luc Carl, who managed and tended bar at a nightclub called St. Jerome's. According to Starland, Lady Gaga was smitten with Carl, but he didn't always seem to share her feelings. Starland says he treated her badly, mocking her taste in music and being unfaithful to her. Their

Musical Influence: David Bowie

If you ask Lady Gaga which artist influenced her most, she's likely to say glam rocker David Bowie. Like Lady Gaga, Bowie was an artist who used a wild, over-the-top image to drive his stardom. No outfit or hairstyle was too outlandish. Bowie, like Gaga, loved the attention that came with celebrating strangeness.

Bowie was born January 8, 1947, as David Robert Jones. He rose to fame in the early 1970s, at first under the stage name Ziggy Stardust. In classic glam rock style, appearance is almost as important as sound. Bowie wore heavy makeup; big hair; and off-the-wall, futuristic outfits, although he moved away from this image later in his career.

Over a career spanning four decades, Bowie released more than twenty albums. His biggest hits include 1969's "Space Oddity," 1975's "Young Americans," and 1981's "Under Pressure," for which he collaborated with the band Queen. In 2004 *Rolling Stone* magazine ranked Bowie 39 on its list of the top 100 rockers of all time. Bowie was awarded a Grammy Lifetime Achievement Award in 2006 and continues to perform for his loyal fan base.

Glam: David Bowie performs on his Ziggy Stardust Tour in 1973.

relationship would remain hot and cold for the next several years.

Fusari, who still maintained a professional relationship with Lady Gaga, went to work to find her another label. Meanwhile, Lady Gaga continued to write. Her music, still generally beat-driven and upbeat on the surface, took on some darker notes. Her experiences, both personal and professional, drove her lyrics.

Welcome, Gaga: Lady Gaga performs with Lady Gaga and the Starlight Revue at Chicago's Lallapalooza festival in 2007. Lady Starlight (not pictured) was operating the turntables behind Gaga.

World, Meet Lady Gaga

Lady Gaga was crushed after Def Jam dropped her, but Fusari kept working to find her a record label. He called Vincent Herbert, a friend who ran his own record label, Da Family (later renamed Streamline), which was a part of Interscope Records. He asked Herbert for a favor and got Lady Gaga an audition with Interscope. Many of Interscope's artists relied on others to write

their songs. The label wanted Lady Gaga to prove she could write good songs. They gave her a musical track and told her to write the lyrics to fit it. She worked hard on the song, which would eventually become "The Fame" and appear on her debut album.

With these lyrics, Lady Gaga had passed the test. She was signed to Streamline, as well as to several other labels under the Interscope umbrella (group of companies). Interscope didn't see Lady Gaga as a star, though. They liked her voice but didn't think that she had the look of a pop star. Her main role with the label, they believed, would be as a songwriter.

It may not have been exactly what Lady Gaga had in mind, but it was a start. She got to work, writing both for herself and for other artists—from Britney Spears to Fergie to the New Kids on the Block. She also wrote for the Pussycat Dolls, an all-female group known for their burlesque-style stage shows. Often Lady Gaga also provided reference vocals as well. This means that she would sing the songs and record them so that the stars would know how they went. One of the songs

"Quicksand"

One of the songs Lady Gaga wrote in 2007 was for Britney Spears, an artist Lady Gaga had grown up admiring. The song, titled "Quicksand," appeared on Spears's 2008 album *Circus*. Originally, Lady Gaga had wanted the song for her own album, but Interscope thought it worked better for Spears. "It was awesome seeing the song change when [Spears] put her touches on it," Lady Gaga said. "I'm just really grateful that she loves the music and she's so supportive of me. She's a fan of my stuff and to write a song that she loves and to know she loves me as an artist, you can't ask for anything better than that."

Voices: Thousands of fans turned out to listen to Amy Winehouse *(above)* at Lallapalooza in Chicago in 2007. About two hundred fans listened to Lady Gaga perform.

she wrote for the Pussycat Dolls was titled "Money Honey." But the final product was so uniquely Lady Gaga that she ended up keeping it for herself.

Lollapalooza 2007

Lady Gaga's manager, Laurent Besencon, was taking a more active role in Lady Gaga's career. He was slowly pushing Fusari out. Lady Gaga wasn't complaining, though, after Besencon secured her a place at Lollapalooza, one of the biggest and most famous music festivals in the world. Lollapalooza features both big-name talent as well as up-and-coming artists. In August 2007, Lady Gaga headed to Chicago, Illinois, the U.S. home for the festival, hoping to make a name for herself. She took with her a friend from high school and Lady Starlight, as her on-stage DJ, playing records to back up Lady Gaga's vocals and dancing.

Of course, an unknown twenty-year-old artist wouldn't get top billing at such a major concert. But Lollapalooza features multiple stages. Much of the audience sticks to the big stage, where the major acts perform. In 2007 Lollapalooza's big acts included Pearl Jam,

Muse, and Kings of Leon. Other fans were at the second stage, where smaller—but still well-established—artists such as the Black Keys, Amy Winehouse, and Snow Patrol performed. Finally, several small stages featured unknown up-and-comers such as Lady Gaga.

Lady Gaga's set on August 4 didn't go the way she'd hoped. First, she was constantly being mistaken for British singer-songwriter Amy Winehouse. Gaga got so tired of being mistaken for Winehouse that

An estimated seventy-five thousand fans turned out for the Lollapalooza music festival in Chicago on August 4, 2007. Of these, only about two hundred actually took in Lady Gaga's set. While that might seem like a tiny number, it was still the largest crowd in front of which she'd ever performed.

A Lost Friendship

As Lady Gaga's fame—and checkbook—grew, she heard from an old friend, Wendy Starland. At first, Lady Gaga was thrilled to hear from Starland. She thanked her again for introducing her to Fusari and helping to kick-start her career. But then the conversation took a cooler turn. Starland asked Lady Gaga if she would compensate her for the role she'd played in her career. Lady Gaga bristled at the idea. She didn't believe someone should be paid simply for introducing an artist to a producer, and she told Starland so. At one point, Starland threatened to sue Lady Gaga, though she didn't go through with it. Starland never got any money, and the friendship between the women was effectively over.

Platinum: Lady Gaga performs as a blonde for the first time on October 4, 2007, in New York.

soon after the festival, she dyed her hair platinum blonde—a look she has kept ever since. She was given almost no time to set up and prepare for her set. Then, onstage, the table that Lady Starlight used for the record player was uneven, causing the record to constantly skip. Despite all the problems, Lady Gaga worked through her performance, drawing heavily on her burlesque background. It was racy and over-the-top and was received with mixed reactions. "That was not a performance I choose to really remember so fondly," she later said.

Lady Gaga was furious. She felt as if she'd been set up to fail. The next day, she fired Besencon. She also told Lady Starlight that her days as DJ were over (she instead asked Starlight to serve as her stylist).

Back to the Studio

Lady Gaga went back to writing and recording, hoping to impress the executives at Interscope. She worked a lot with a producer called Akon. He was one of the few at the company who really saw the potential in Lady Gaga.

One Sunday afternoon late in 2007, Akon and Interscope cofounder Jimmy Iovine were listening to some of the Interscope's unreleased

material. They came to a track Lady Gaga had recorded, titled "Boys Boys Boys." The song—an answer to an old Motley Crue rock song titled "Girls, Girls, Girls"—grabbed Iovine's attention. It has an upbeat tempo and a catchy tune, and it sounds like something he might hear on the radio. He asked Akon's opinion. Akon, having long been a supporter of Lady Gaga's, was quick to agree. Just like that, Iovine was sold on Lady Gaga.

According to one source, Iovine called Lady Gaga that very day. He told her, "Stefani, Gaga, whatever—I just want you to know that we really like this song of yours and we're going to be behind you."

It was big news for Lady Gaga. Having Iovine's support meant that Interscope was ready to think of her not just as a songwriter but as an artist worthy of the label's time and investment. Interscope had her sign with Akon's label, Kon Live Distribution, and it was finally time to put an album together. Lady Gaga, RedOne, Akon, and others got to work recording and choosing songs for her first major release.

Support: Posing for a picture in 2009 are, from left, Akon; Doug Morris, chairman and CEO of Universal Music Group; Lady Gaga; and Jimmy Iovine, chairman of Interscope. Gaga caught the attention of Iovine and Akon in late 2007.

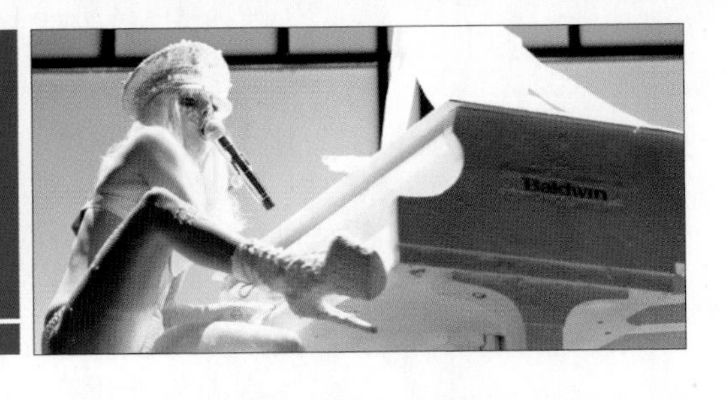

December 9, 2009

What artists are winning in this digital decade?

From the Pages of USA TODAY

CDs sagged as music downloads rocketed. *USA TODAY*'s Edna Gundersen assesses fresh data on the decade's digital revolution.

Top digital songs

Artist, Track, Sales in millions
Flo Rida, "Low" 5.2
Lady Gaga, "Just Dance" 4.7
Jason Mraz, "I'm Yours" 4.6
Timbaland/OneRepublic, "Apologize" 4.4
Black Eyed Peas, "Boom Boom Pow" 4.3
Soulja Boy, "Crank That" 4.3
Lady Gaga, "Poker Face" 4.2
Coldplay, "Viva La Vida" 4.1
Taylor Swift, "Love Story" 4.0
Katy Perry, "Hot N Cold" 3.9

Rapper Flo Rida's "Low," last year's raw ode to a nightclub "shawty," holds title as the top-selling digital song of the past 10 years, with 5.2 million paid downloads, according to Nielsen SoundScan, which began tabulating track sales in July 2003.

Things were moving very fast. It was a whirlwind of activity. Lady Gaga and RedOne worked on some of the older songs she'd already recorded. They also recorded some new ones, including "Just Dance" and "Poker Face."

At the same time, Lady Gaga was revising her look. She had recently dyed her hair blonde. She was gravitating more toward

All of the decade's top 10 digital songs were released since 2007, eight in the past two years, evidence of downloading's explosive growth as music consumers shift away from full CDs to single digital tracks.

Fans have paid for 1.1 billion tracks so far in 2009, compared with 963 million in the equivalent period in 2008. This year, four artists have broken the single-year digital record set by Rihanna, who sold 9.9 million tracks in 2008.

Artist Sales in millions
Lady Gaga 13.6
Michael Jackson 11.6
Black Eyed Peas 11.1
Taylor Swift 10.7

Top digital albums
Album, Copies
Coldplay, *Viva La Vida* 751,000
Soundtrack for *Twilight* 533,000
Taylor Swift, *Fearless* 494,000
Kings of Leon, *Only By the Night* 481,000
John Mayer, *Continuum* 428,000
Daughtry, *Daughtry* 382,000

Digital albums, while still a less popular format than CDs or digital singles, continue to boom. "As the consumer becomes more comfortable downloading, you're going to see an increased importance placed on the digital album," says Eric Weinberg, president of Nielsen Entertainment. "The older consumer tends to be more comfortable purchasing physical music. That's going to change over time as the means to access music electronically becomes easier and more secure."

—Edna Gundersen

elaborate, European-style fashion. The look was often complemented with short, tight shorts and very high heels. The sound and the look were coming together quickly, and the artist that was emerging had Akon excited. "She's brave, she's fresh, she's different," he said. "You gotta take her as she is, and that's the beauty of it."

IN FOCUS

Musical Influence: Boy George

Lady Gaga has often pointed to British pop star Boy George as an inspiration for her music and style. Boy George, born George Alan O'Dowd on June 14, 1961, is an openly gay singer known as much for his androgynous style (having both male and female characteristics) as for his music. In the early 1980s, he fronted the band Culture Club. The band released four albums that decade (and a reunion album in 1999). Their biggest hit was "Karma Chameleon." It reached No. 1 in sixteen countries, including the United States, where it spent three weeks at the top of the charts. Culture Club broke up in 1986, and Boy George went on to a solo career, releasing eight solo albums. As a solo artist, Boy George enjoyed little chart success in the United States. His only Top 20 hit was 1992's "The Crying Game," which peaked at No. 15.

Style: Boy George performs with the Culture Club in 1983.

Just Dance

As the album, which would be titled *The Fame*, took shape, Akon remained Lady Gaga's greatest ally. Her sound was unique, unlike anything else the label was producing. Some executives at Interscope didn't like that. They thought her sound wasn't mainstream and urged her to change it. Akon wouldn't hear of it. He stood by Lady Gaga, and together they made the album the way *they* wanted it made.

In late 2007, Lady Gaga moved to Los Angeles, California, where she helped to finalize *The Fame*. She surrounded herself with people

whom she called the Haus of Gaga—stylists, producers, musicians, dancers, and anyone who she felt could contribute to her creative process. Among them was a new boyfriend, stylist Matthew Williams.

Lady Gaga and Interscope agreed that her first single should be "Just Dance." It was a carefully considered choice. The song didn't have the same depth of lyrics as many of the other tracks on the album. But it did have one undeniable strength: it was catchy. The single was released on April 8, 2008, and Lady Gaga appeared in clubs around the country to promote it. She also filmed her first video, which she described as fun but very humbling in its scope and high profile.

Lady Gaga later described the appeal of the song. "To me there is nothing more powerful than one song that you can put on in a room anywhere in the world and somebody gets up and dances. That's what pop is, it resonates on a visceral [gut] level."

Electric: This picture from 2008 was used to promote Lady Gaga's song "Just Dance." The music video for this song features Gaga with a lightning bolt under her eye.

"Just Dance" wasn't an instant hit on mainstream radio. But it quickly became a sensation on the club scene. With its catchy beat and lyrics, it seemed tailor-made to thump through the speakers in nightclubs worldwide. Suddenly, people started wondering just who this new artist with the quirky name was. The

February 15, 2010

Lady Gaga makes AIDS awareness her cause

From the Pages of USA TODAY

Defy Lady Gaga, and you might unleash the fame monster within. The idiosyncratic Grammy-winning performer (real name: Stefani Germanotta) put the kibosh on [didn't allow] still photos during a recent media appearance. One bystander didn't get the memo and snapped an illicit shot.

"Can you erase that, please?" Gaga says, turning to face the interviewer. "I'm so sorry. Could we have privacy? This is not a time for people to be taking photos. It's such a serious conversation. I like to give you my full attention."

Gaga, 23, has joined singer Cyndi Lauper to promote safe sex as one of the faces of MAC cosmetics' Viva Glam campaign, which supports people living with HIV/AIDS.

"I have a tremendous relationship with the gay community. When people find out I'm doing this, they say, 'Is it because of your relationship with the gay community, because you want to speak out about AIDS?' And I say no," Gaga explains.

single, which would later take off on mainstream radio and eventually reach No.1 on the *Billboard* Hot 100 chart, went on to sell more than 3 million copies. Lady Gaga even got to perform it live at the Miss Universe Pageant in 2008.

Touring with the New Kids

Lady Gaga was ready to capitalize on her growing fame. At Interscope's instruction, she went on tour as the opening act for the reunion of the early-'90s boy band New Kids on the Block. It was an uncomfortable

"AIDS is not a gay disease. That's part of what I want to accomplish . . . really raise awareness of what AIDS is today."

Gaga says she wants to use her fame for good.

"People look up to you for your success and your voice in the world. My message as a woman, to my fans, is always: Love yourself, free yourself, be whoever you want to be."

She's appearing in the Viva Glam ad campaign and lending her name to a new lipstick. "I'm a girl's girl. I'm kind of rough around the edges, too. Believe it or not, I do think about what's appropriate," Gaga says.

Despite a busy touring schedule, Gaga says, she makes time for causes.

"This work is important to me. They are a breath of fresh air for me. You'll never see me at a nightclub doing my thing to get a bunch of money to make an appearance. I'd much rather use that time to sleep/do work like this."

—Donna Freydkin

Awareness: This 2010 ad for MAC cosmetics, featuring Cyndi Lauper *(left)* and Lady Gaga, was used to raise awareness about AIDS.

pairing, in personality and style. The New Kids had been *the* boy band of the early 1990s, and their audience then was mainly preteen and teenaged girls. So by 2008, most of their audience was women in their thirties, and the band's appeal was nostalgia. Lady Gaga, meanwhile, was edgy and new. She didn't sing the brand of bubblegum pop that had made the New Kids famous. This led to some clashes. The New Kids didn't like her act. It was too showy, too over-the-top. Lady Gaga tried to tone it down, understanding who her audience was, but she had to be herself. Every night, she'd ask the New Kids if she could join them onstage to sing one of the songs she'd written for them.

But only once did they ever take her up on her offer.

Lady Gaga was enjoying her growing success, but it came at a price. She was working constantly. It was more than just the shows. She constantly promoted herself, doing interviews, meeting with record executives, greeting fans, writing new music, rehearsing, sitting in wardrobe or makeup, and just generally being as hands-on as she could. Those close to her said she was lucky if she got four hours of sleep a night. She would keep going until she was exhausted. Then she'd crash, have to cancel a show, and start the cycle over again.

USA TODAY Snapshots®

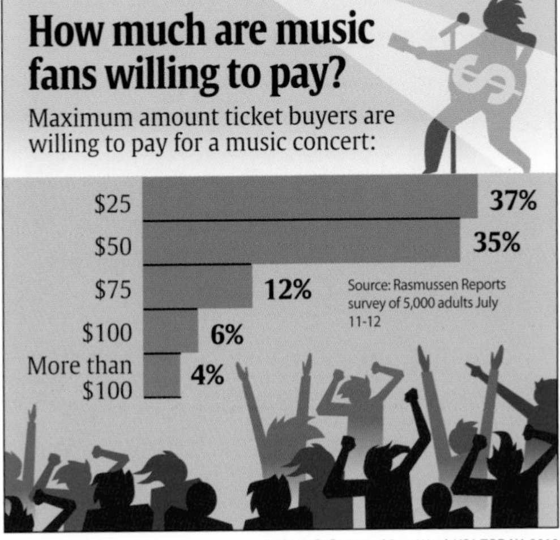

By Anne R. Carey and Sam Ward, USA TODAY, 2010

Media rounds: As she built her career, Lady Gaga *(front right)* worked all the time. She did lots of interviews, including this one on MTV's *TRL* in 2008.

Her short relationship with stylist Matthew Williams ended. Those close to Lady Gaga said she seemed desperately

lonely. She couldn't stand to be alone. She didn't even want to be by herself when she slept. So Angela Ciemny, the wife of Lady Gaga's tour manager David Ciemny, often crashed with Lady Gaga.

None of that came through in her public persona, however. Her fashion style (she often dressed in very few clothes), suggestive dance moves, and outspoken nature caused many to compare her to a young Madonna. She pushed the limits. She spoke out about controversial subjects such as gay rights and proudly proclaimed that she was bisexual. In part because of her style and her political views, Lady Gaga was gaining an increasing following among the gay community. She later credited this loyal fan base with being a big part of getting her recognized and played on the radio. Things were moving fast for Lady Gaga, and they were about to get even faster.

Hit: Lady Gaga performs in December 2008 wearing her trademark *Fame* crystal sunglasses. *The Fame* album reached No. 1 in several countries and rose to No. 4 on the U.S. charts.

The Fame

Finally, in August 2008, Lady Gaga and Interscope released *The Fame*. For many new artists, the release of a debut album is a low-key affair, without much fanfare. But Lady Gaga's early success with "Just Dance" had put *The Fame* on the music industry's radar. Many reviewers seemed to know that this wasn't just another debut album. They sensed it was the first album from a new force in the music industry.

Billboard wrote, "*The Fame* proves [Lady Gaga is] more than one hit and a bag of stage

Pet projects drop by about a third
9,297 'earmarks' for 2010 spending bills cost $10.2B

tricks." Meanwhile, Alexis Petridis of the British newspaper the *Guardian* said, "Virtually everything on *The Fame* arrives packing an immensely addictive melody or an inescapable hook, virtually everything sounds like another hit single." However, in the very same review, Petridis described Lady Gaga's music as "shameless pop music. . . it's hard not to feel that you've heard a lot of this before." Jamie Gill of Yahoo! Music called *The Fame* "a sparkling pop album crammed with infectious melodies that you somehow never, ever want to hear again."

The Fame would go on to reach No. 1 in several countries, including the United Kingdom, Canada, and Germany. It peaked at No. 4 in the United States.

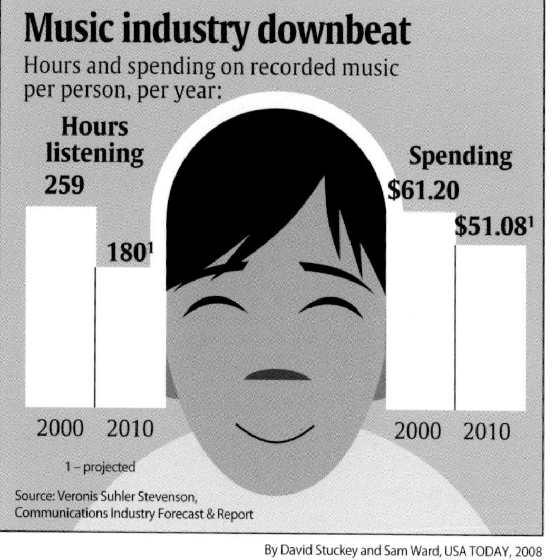

By David Stuckey and Sam Ward, USA TODAY, 2008

"Poker Face"

In September 2008, Interscope released a second single. At first, the plan had been to release "Beautiful, Dirty Rich," but Lady Gaga and her label later changed their minds and went with "Poker Face." It turned out to be a brilliant decision. While "Just Dance" had been catchy and sexy, "Poker Face" was downright infectious. Almost overnight, it was blaring on pop radio stations across the world. "Poker Face" proved that Lady Gaga was no one-hit wonder. Despite its upbeat tempo, the song showed a much darker side as well. Lady Gaga was singing about putting on a false appearance. In the game of poker,

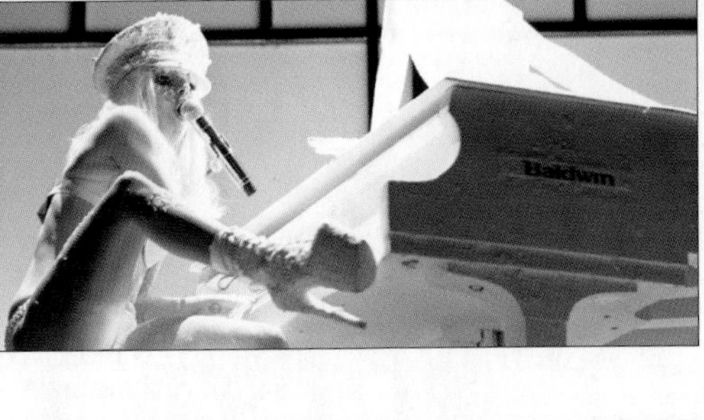

June 12, 2009

Lady Gaga Feels the Fame

From the Pages of USA TODAY

In the landscape that is pop culture, Lady Gaga so far defies categorization. "Shy" is one label she certainly would not wear.

The 23-year-old performer of danceable synth-pop rocked the cover of *Rolling Stone* in a dress made of bubbles recently. Lately, Lady Gaga is getting as much attention for her candor as for her music and cutting-edge costumes. As for her propensity for discussing [her bisexuality], she says: "I don't think being gay or being bisexual or being sexually free is anything that should be hidden. Everybody has a right to their secrecy, of course, but I don't feel particularly shy about it. It is who I am.

"I sing very openly about it in my music, so I suppose I could say that I choose not to hide it in interviews because I don't care to hide it. . . ."

Lady Gaga's 2008 debut album, *The Fame*, has gone platinum—and remains No. 8 on the Billboard 200 chart—and her first single, "Just Dance," became just the fifth song to sell 4 million downloads. (Singles "Poker Face" and "LoveGame" are Nos. 5 and 6 on *Billboard*'s Hot 100.)

A former New York University art student who lists influences such as Andy Warhol, David Bowie, Prince, and Madonna in her album credits, Gaga (her name comes from the Queen song "Radio Ga Ga") began writing songs for acts such as the Pussycat Dolls. She originally was signed by Def Jam; R&B artist Akon and Interscope's Jimmy Iovine, signed her after she was dropped, and released *The Fame*.

Her unique '80s-esque dance music has been embraced by the gay and hip-hop

a player tries to keep a neutral facial expression, so as not to give away hand strength (the cards he or she is holding). Lady Gaga was singing about doing the same thing in life—about presenting an outward appearance that doesn't reflect what is really going on inside. She later said that the song was about hiding her own bisexuality.

community alike. "Those are two very different communities, but something they both share is love of celebration," she says. "My relationship with the gay community is long-standing and loyal, and I love them very much. I consider my music to be very gay, and I love that it is gay."

As for her hip-hop acceptance, Kanye West is planning a fall tour in which Lady Gaga will co-headline and perform with him. "It is very exciting," she says. "He is extremely talented, and I think it truly shows his relevance as a pioneer that he has taken such a new artist under his wing to share the stage."

Currently in Tokyo performing and doing interviews, Gaga also is working on a rerelease of *The Fame* as well as new material.

Though it may be early in her career for comparisons, many have likened her to Madonna.

"I'm very flattered. She has always been completely unique and original," Gaga says. "That is something I aspire for. I hope to have a very similar conversation with you maybe 30 years from now when we are talking about another album of mine."

—Mike Snider

Float on: Lady Gaga performs in concert in a dress made of bubbles in May 2009. She wore a more risqué bubble outfit for the cover of *Rolling Stone* in June 2009.

Chris Williams of *Billboard* was one of many who heaped praise upon the song. He wrote, "Once again, hooks are aplenty, with '80s-inspired synthesizers, robotic verses and a warm, sunny hook in the chorus, which is even more addictive than the previous single ["Just Dance"]. . . . While comparisons abound—Christina Aguilera, Gwen Stefani, Madonna—Lady Gaga has a singular [unique] sound and style.

IN FOCUS

Musical Influence: Grace Jones

Many music experts have noted the strong influence of Jamaican American musician, actress, and model Grace Jones on Lady Gaga—both in her sound and her style. Jones, born May 18, 1948, burst onto the music scene in the late 1970s with a dance-friendly pop sound and an androgynous look. Between 1977 and 2008, she released eleven albums. Her distinctive contralto (deep), talking-style voice and trademark flat-top hairstyle made her one of the biggest names in new age rock of the late 1970s and early 1980s. Her popularity was highest in Europe, where she had several Top 10 albums. Although she was very popular in the American gay community, she never caught on as a mainstream artist in the United States. Her most successful album on U.S. charts was 1981's *Nightclubbing*, which peaked at No. 32.

Strong: Grace Jones, pictured here in the 1980s, had an androgynous look.

With a focused artistic vision, a swagger in her interview style and above all, a fantastic collection of diverse pop nuggets, Gaga is playing her cards right—and 'Poker' is another obvious ace."

"Poker Face" was a massive hit. It topped the charts in the United States and more than twenty other countries. Lady Gaga became the first artist since Christina Aguilera to reach No. 1 with her first two singles.

Soon Lady Gaga and Aguilera would be linked in a very different way. Over the years, Lady Gaga had continued to refine a truly one-of-a-kind sense of style. Her outfits demanded attention. She became famous for wearing tight skirts, dresses, and leotards—rarely pants—that

accentuated her sexy, feminine figure. In fact, for one outing, she didn't bother to wear a skirt at all, choosing instead to wear only a leather jacket and gloves over underwear and fishnet stockings. The look was completed with black sunglasses and platform ankle-high boots. Big sunglasses and high-heeled footwear—along with Gaga's straightened platinum blonde hair with long bangs, bright red lipstick, and colorful eye shadow—were a signature look. In late 2008, some people started noticing that Aguilera had suddenly adopted a very similar style for her music video "Not Myself Tonight."

Aguilera clearly was unhappy with the accusation. "This person [Lady Gaga] was just brought to my attention not too long ago," Aguilera answered. "I'm not quite sure who this person is, to be honest. I don't know if it is a man or a woman. I just wasn't sure."

Look-alikes: *Left*: Christina Aguilera performs at the MTV Video Music Awards in September 2008. *Right*: Lady Gaga performs at a summer concert series in May 2008. Many people thought Christina Aguilera was copying Lady Gaga's style.

Aguilera's comments made big news. Many saw them as insincere. They believed that she had indeed copied Lady Gaga and that she was unhappy at having been called out on it. If she had simply said that Lady Gaga had inspired an outfit or two, the story would likely have disappeared. But instead, it grew into a small-scale entertainment scandal. Lady Gaga was already getting plenty of media attention for both her music and her style. But a perceived feud with one of pop's biggest stars only helped to spread Gaga's name.

Lady Gaga has always been sharp about marketing herself. "It was very flattering when it happened," she said of Aguilera's alleged

Internet Marketing

Lady Gaga is often praised as a marketing genius. Even before she was a star, she understood the importance of the Internet in building a fan base. As a little-known artist trying to make it big, Lady Gaga's marketing campaign started out small. She put songs on social networking websites, most notably MySpace. She also kept and regularly maintained a Facebook profile. She paid an online music service to feature her work. And she sent audio and video clips to popular music bloggers. One blogger who helped build Lady Gaga's career is Perez Hilton. Hilton blogged about Lady Gaga in June 2008, just as "Just Dance" was starting to gain some traction.

Online: Blogger Perez Hilton *(right)* helped Lady Gaga gain popularity.

mimicking of her style. "She's a huge star and if anything, I should send her flowers because a lot of people in America didn't know who I was until that whole thing happened. It really put me on the map in a way, though of course, I don't want to be remembered for the Christina Aguilera scandal. What it showed me was, even though I've only been on the commercial market for seven or eight months, I've really burned graphic images of my visuals onto the irises [a part of the eye] of my fans."

Hitting the Road

Lady Gaga had the attention of the entertainment world, and she wasn't about to let that go. She worked hard to promote her album. She appeared on television shows including *The Tonight Show with Jay Leno*, *American Idol*, and *So You Think You Can Dance*? She gave countless interviews. But even though she was very willing to put herself out there, she also had managed to craft a sense of mystery about herself. Few fans knew her real name. She tried to keep her background somewhat secret. Of course, in the Internet age, this is a nearly impossible task. But she managed it well.

Television: Lady Gaga performs on *The Tonight Show with Jay Leno* in January 2009 to promote her album, *The Fame*.

Lady Gaga also hit the road again. First up was a

Lots of ladies: The Pussycat Dolls perform in the United Kingdom on January 25, 2009. Lady Gaga opened for the girl group on this three-week tour and stole a lot of the attention.

three-week tour of the United Kingdom with the Pussycat Dolls. The tour started on January 18, 2009, in Aberdeen, Scotland. Lady Gaga was a supporting act for the Dolls, but she was soon stealing most of the attention.

Even the headliners of the show were realizing that they were being upstaged. "I remember watching [Lady Gaga] perform," said Nicole Scherzinger, lead singer of the Pussycat Dolls. "I looked at her and said, 'I'm afraid of her.' As an artist, there are things I want to be fearless enough to communicate, but I limit myself sometimes. She had no boundaries, no fear, and did it in such a creative, theatrical way. She inspired me to be like, 'Wow, you can do this.'"

The Fame Ball Tour

By March 2009, Lady Gaga was back in the United States and set to begin a new tour. But this time, she wouldn't be a supporting act. She would be the headliner. The Fame Ball Tour began March 12 at the House of Blues in San Diego, California, and continued through the

end of September. It included stops in North America, Europe, and Asia.

Lady Gaga stressed that the Fame Ball was more than just a music concert. She considered it to be a traveling museum of pop art. This art form arose in the 1950s and focused on highlighting mass-produced items from advertising, comics, and other popular forums. A famous example of pop art is Andy Warhol's painting of Campbell Soup cans, for example. Lady Gaga described the show: "It's not really a tour, it's more of a traveling party," she said. "I want it to be an entire experience from [the] minute you walk in [the] front door to [the] minute I begin to sing. And when it's all over, everyone's going to press rewind and relive it again. It's going to be as if you're walking into New York circa 1974. There's an art installation in the lobby, a DJ spinning your favorite records in the main room, and then the most haunting performance that you've ever seen on the stage."

More than music: The audience takes pictures as Lady Gaga performs during her Fame Ball Tour on March 13, 2009, in Los Angeles, California. She thought of this tour as a traveling museum of pop art.

Gaga's Teacup

Sometime in early 2009, Lady Gaga began carrying a little purple teacup and saucer with her everywhere she went. She claimed that it held ginger tea, which is good for the vocal cords. People—especially the British media—became fascinated with the teacup. It was such an odd thing, they noted, for a grown woman to carry a teacup with her to dinner, to television interviews, and everywhere else. The teacup even got its own Facebook page!

Another time, an interviewer noticed that Lady Gaga didn't have the teacup and asked about it. "She [the teacup] hasn't got a name," Lady Gaga answered. "But she's quite famous now, so I made her stay in today. I take her everywhere because she makes me feel at home."

Tea time: Lady Gaga leaves her hotel in Britain in April 2009 carrying a purple teacup and saucer. For a while, Lady Gaga carried this teacup everywhere.

Lady Gaga split her performance into four parts, with a video separating each part. She even came out onstage calling herself "Candy Warhol," a play on the name of pop art pioneer Andy Warhol, one of Lady Gaga's idols. It was a highly choreographed show complete with multiple outfit changes for its star. The most famous of these outfits was made entirely of plastic bubbles—an outfit that she proudly donned for the May 2009 cover of *Rolling Stone* magazine.

Lady Gaga was always eager to remind people that her show

contained no lip synching. Many performers who have heavy dance routines in their shows prerecord their vocals and move their lips to the lyrics as they dance. This lip synching allows them to save their breath for the demanding dance moves. But Lady Gaga would have none of that. Fans were paying top dollar to hear her sing, and she wasn't going to give them something prerecorded. She also avoided the use of Auto-Tune, an instrument that corrects or modulates pitch in a vocal performance. (Many music experts consider Auto-Tune to be a way for less skilled vocalists to cover their shortcomings.)

One of the highlights of the tour was supposed to have been the Glastonbury Festival of Contemporary Performing Arts in the United Kingdom in June 2009. Glastonbury is a huge music festival, and Lady Gaga was excited to perform before the massive audiences it attracted. But on June 25, the day before Lady Gaga was scheduled to perform, the news of pop legend Michael Jackson's death broke. Lady Gaga was crushed. She had been a big fan, and her friend RedOne had worked with Jackson. According to some, Lady Gaga was so upset by the news that she refused to leave her tour bus the entire day. She came out the next day and gave a performance that had festivalgoers—mainly rock fans, not pop fans—buzzing. Most notably, they were talking about the black bra she wore. Equipped with special

Sparks: Many people talked about Lady Gaga's black bra which shot fireworks. Here, she wears it while performing in Canada on June 21, 2009.

Intersexed Gaga?

In early 2009, a rumor began to circulate, claiming that Lady Gaga is an intersexed individual—a person whose internal and external organs are not of the same sex. In June 2009, a photograph of Lady Gaga taken at Glastonbury appeared to show evidence of this. Internet message boards buzzed with the news. In an online quote, Lady Gaga admitted it was true—though where the quote actually came from or whether it was genuine, nobody knew for sure.

Many fans believed that the entire rumor was another example of Lady Gaga creating a media stir, much as she'd done with the teacup earlier in the year. After all, they pointed out, Lady Gaga had performed countless shows over the past year in little more than her underwear. It was obvious she didn't have anything to hide. Later, in a televised interview with journalist Barbara Walters, Lady Gaga said the rumors of her intersexed gender identity were untrue.

pyrotechnic features, the bra shot fireworks from the caged cups of the bra, wowing her audience.

Loneliness

The tour was grueling. Lady Gaga was working crazy hours and getting very little sleep. But she refused to scale back. She continued to push herself until, at one point, she became so sick from fatigue that she had to cancel everything for three days to recover. Afterward, she was asked what the low point in her year had been. "Loneliness, being on the road," she answered. "I have a chronic sadness that recurs. The lowest point was in Australia, in May. I was overwhelmingly sad and I didn't know why because I had all these things to be happy about." Lady Gaga added that she used the powerful emotions of sadness and loneliness to write the song "Speechless," which would be featured on her next album.

Lonely: Lady Gaga is pictured in her "LoveGame" outfit in Australia on May 21, 2009. Lady Gaga remembers being extremely sad during this time period.

By the time the Fame Ball Tour was over in September, Lady Gaga had performed sixty-nine shows in front of mostly sold-out crowds. Media reviews were generally favorable. Christopher Muther of the *Boston Globe* wrote, "The combination of song and spectacle was crowd-pleasing and exhilarating. Her club-ready songs were delivered by a woman who is clearly studied, intelligent, and talented." Whitney Pastorek of *Entertainment Weekly*, however, described the onstage antics—from flaming bras to the dramatic stage show that accompanied the music—as "at times a bit silly." But he went on to acknowledge, "For all her cocky bluster, perhaps the most undeniable aspect of Gaga's talent is this: The girl can, and does, sing."

Staying on Top

While Lady Gaga was on tour, she released two more singles in North America. The first, "LoveGame," reached No. 5 on *Billboard*'s Hot 100 chart. Next came "Paparazzi," which had been cowritten by Fusari before he and Lady Gaga went their separate ways. Like her first two hits, it came with a catchy, danceable beat—Alexis Petridis of the *Guardian* said that the tune "takes up residence in your brain and refuses to budge."

Lady Gaga explained that "Paparazzi" was inspired both by her personal quest for fame and by the difficulties of balancing fame with a personal love life. It reached No. 6 on *Billboard*'s Hot 100 chart, making Lady Gaga only the fourth female artist to chart four Top 10 songs from a debut album. Lady Gaga was in good company—the other names on that list were Christina Aguilera, Fergie, and Beyoncé.

If any doubt remained about Lady Gaga's emergence as a pop sensation, her night at the 2009 MTV Video Music Awards erased it. Lady Gaga took home three awards, including Best New Artist, and electrified the crowd with her graphic performance of "Paparazzi." The performance, in which Lady Gaga acted out a suicide by hanging, was a source of controversy. Many called her onstage antics tasteless, and some even accused her of romanticizing suicide. Lady Gaga casually dismissed the accusations, saying that the faked suicide was supposed to represent the way the paparazzi had killed her private life.

Papa-paparazzi: Lady Gaga poses for a photo promoting her single "Paparazzi" in June 2009. The song is about Gaga's struggle to balance fame with her personal life.

Creative duo: Kanye West *(left)* and Lady Gaga *(right)* attend a party in 2009. The two announced they would tour together, but shortly after the announcement, the tour was canceled.

Also in September, Lady Gaga and hip-hop star Kanye West announced that they would co-headline a new tour, called the Fame Kills Tour. But shortly after the announcement, the tour was canceled. No official reason was given, but some industry experts said that extremely high ticket prices were resulting in low sales. Additionally, West had recently become the center of a controversy after he crashed the stage to cut off teen singer Taylor Swift as she was accepting her award for Best Female Video at the VMAs. West felt Beyoncé should have won the award.

Lady Gaga shrugged off the controversy. She liked West and respected him as an artist. With the tour canceled, Lady Gaga turned to giving her fans what they wanted—new music. This would also give her the chance to focus solely on promoting her new material.

CHAPTER SIX

Big name: Lady Gaga speaks at the National Equality March on October 11, 2009, in Washington, D.C. Lady Gaga has a large gay following, and, at the event, she spoke about advancing gay rights.

Monster Follow-Up

In October 2009, Lady Gaga headed to Washington, D.C., for the Human Rights Campaign National Dinner. The dinner is a fund-raiser for the Human Rights Campaign, an organization that works for equal rights for lesbian, gay, bisexual, and transgender people. President Barack Obama was also at the event. When he got a chance to speak, he joked, "It's a privilege to be here tonight to open for Lady Gaga. I've made it."

Lady Gaga, who normally revels in being over the top and outrageous, took a more understated approach to the evening. She wore a long black dress and dark glasses and told the audience, "In the music industry, there's still a tremendous amount of accommodation of homophobia [fear of homosexuals], so I'm taking a stand." She then sang a modified version of John Lennon's classic song "Imagine." She'd changed the lyrics to make reference to a college student, Matthew Shepard, who had been beaten and killed in Wyoming in 1998 because he was gay.

Later, at the National Equality March, she spoke again, challenging President Obama to do still more to advance the cause of gay rights. Lady Gaga had always had a large following among the gay community. With appearances such as these, she became a public champion of gay rights.

New Album, New Single

Many young stars who gain fame rapidly aren't ready for all the pressure that comes with overnight stardom. It's easy for them to lose the drive that brought them success in the first place. But that wasn't a problem for Lady Gaga. Just as she hadn't wanted to be a one-hit wonder, she didn't want to be a one-album wonder either. She told interviewers that she planned to be around—and relevant—for the next twenty-five years. But she also understood that staying power takes hard work. And so, even during the long days of the Fame Ball Tour, Lady Gaga never stopped writing. By the end of 2009, she had a whole new group of songs to give her fans. In November she released *The Fame Monster*, a deluxe edition of *The Fame* with eight new songs. Each of the new songs was about an emotional monster born of one of Lady Gaga's fears—such as the fears of love, loneliness, and death. The monsters symbolized the drawbacks of being famous.

"I wrote about everything I didn't write about on *The Fame*," Lady Gaga said. "While traveling the world for two years, I've encountered several monsters, each represented by a different song on the new

record. . . . I wrote every piece on the road—no songs about money, no songs about fame."

The first new single, titled "Bad Romance," featured the paranoia monster. The paranoia monster, Lady Gaga explained, had taken over her love life. She didn't think it was possible to balance love and fame. Musically, the song was something of a new direction for Lady Gaga. Reviewers noted that it has a retro feel, sounding like something that could have come out of the 1980s or the 1990s. Lady Gaga said that she had written "Bad Romance" while riding a tour bus through Norway. She had just been to Germany, and the sounds of the techno music played at German clubs had inspired the melody.

To promote her new album and single, Lady Gaga made an appearance on the sketch comedy show *Saturday Night Live (SNL). SNL*'s writers came up with a skit making fun of the idea that pop icon Madonna was jealous of Lady Gaga's success. Madonna liked the idea and came onto the show to do the skit. During the skit's fictional music talk show, Lady Gaga and Madonna are onstage together to perform. The two, dressed almost identically, soon begin to argue, pull at each other's hair, and fight. The skit ends with one of the cohosts urging the two women to kiss and make up.

"Bad Romance" was a huge hit. It debuted at No. 9 on *Billboard's* Hot 100 chart and rose as high as No. 2.

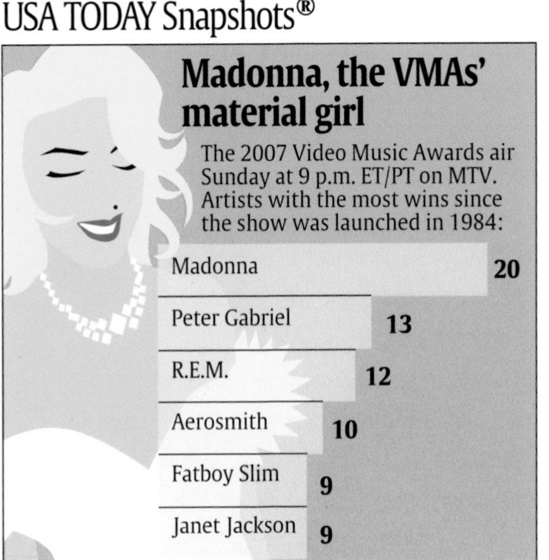

Action packed: Lady Gaga *(left)* and Madonna perform together, while dressed similarly, during the "Deep House Dish" skit on *Saturday Night Live* on October 3, 2009.

The single sold more than one million copies and was, for a time, the most downloaded song on the charts. In the United Kingdom, it became Lady Gaga's third No. 1 hit. The critics seemed to love it as much as the public did. *Rolling Stone* named it one of the top 25 songs of the year. Edna Gundersen of *USA Today* wrote, "[Synthesizer]-powered 'Bad Romance' is a ferocious club thumper with a sordid underbelly." She ranked the song as one of the highlights of the album.

Up in Flames

Lady Gaga was getting more attention than ever. Beyoncé asked Lady Gaga to sing and appear in a video for her song "Video Phone." Lady Gaga gladly accepted. While Lady Gaga said that she enjoyed working with the pop star, the song was generally panned by critics as being repetitive and uninspired. They felt that including Lady Gaga seemed pointless.

IN FOCUS

Musical Influence: Madonna

Ever since Lady Gaga rose to fame, she has been compared to Madonna. It's a comparison that both women have embraced. Madonna was a big influence on young Stefani Germanotta, and in recent years, she has become a Lady Gaga fan, saying that she is "very flattered" by the comparisons.

Madonna Louise Ciccone was born on August 16, 1958. Like Lady Gaga, she started her career by releasing a dance hit, "Everybody." Her self-titled debut album was released in 1983, followed a year later by *Like a Virgin*. Madonna quickly became a pop sensation. Like Lady Gaga, she is provocative, outspoken, politically aware, and distinctly different from any other artist who had come before. She has a style all her own and isn't afraid to show some skin. From 1983 to 2011, Madonna released eleven full-length albums, which sold more than 300 million copies. According to the *Guinness World Records*, she is the top-selling female recording artist of all time.

Provocative: Madonna is pictured at the 1984 MTV Video Music Awards. Lady Gaga is frequently compared to Madonna.

Lady Gaga was also featured heavily at the American Music Awards (AMA) on November 22, 2009. She was nominated for several awards and had also agreed to perform at the ceremony. Although she didn't win any AMAs that night, she still had the crowd buzzing. For her performance, she and her dancers came out dressed in nude bodysuits

(tight-fitting skin-colored suits that give the impression that a person isn't wearing any clothing). Over the bodysuits, Gaga and her dancers wore skeleton helmets, vests, and high-heeled footwear.

Gaga started her performance with a shortened version of "Bad Romance." As the music ended, she picked up a microphone stand, spun around, and ran toward a large piano encased in glass. She smashed the glass with the stand, sending shards everywhere.

Lady Gaga stepped through the broken glass to sit at the piano, which then burst into flames. Surrounded by the flames, she performed "Speechless," an emotionally packed ballad that she'd written for her father, who was having heart problems and avoiding a surgery. The song was her way of asking her father to have the surgery (he did have the surgery, which was successful). Midway through the song, as

Flames: At the 2009 American Music Awards, Lady Gaga performed "Speechless" on a flaming piano. Her father's reluctance to have surgery for a heart condition inspired her to write the song.

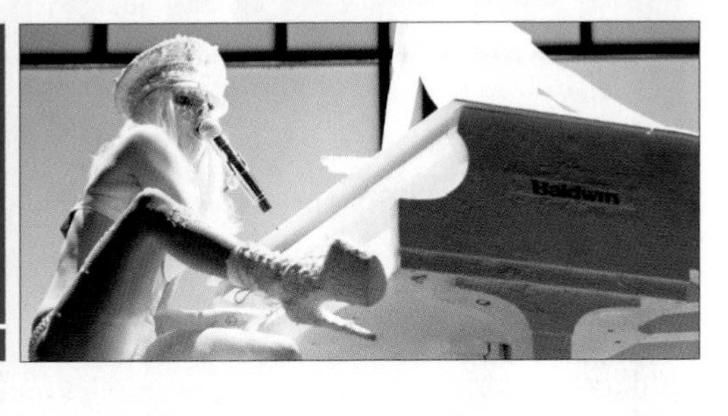

November 24, 2009

Lady Gaga's ice-hearted 'Monster'

From the Pages of USA TODAY

The overnight sensation who went from a Yonkers [New York] lounge act to, well, a fame monster, replenishes her 2008 debut with eight new tracks, delivering a heftier deluxe edition than the usual pop star looking to lure holiday shoppers.

The worthwhile lures? Synth-powered "Bad Romance" is a ferocious club thumper with a sordid underbelly, and the campy, name-dropping "Dance in the Dark," which cops its gabby interlude from Madonna's "Vogue," is a frothy New Wave throwback. Much of the rest sounds like *The Fame* reframed.

Even hip-hop's bling extremists can't match Gaga's naked materialism, yet the Material Girl is less a touchstone on *Monster* than Marilyn Manson, who would admire the dark and decadent lyrics threading these dance rhythms. Self-obsession remains a dominant theme, though it felt as harmless as spray-on glitter throughout *The Fame*'s immersion in sex, partying and celebrity. On *Monster*, Gaga's icy aloofness and seeming aversion to a genuine human connection leave a disturbing void. With an avant-garde intellect, pop-electro eccentricities and freaky theatrics competing for attention, there's no room for heart.

—Edna Gundersen

she belted out, "Would you give it all up? Would you give it all up?" she picked up several glass bottles and angrily smashed them against the burning piano. As the music died away, she is left alone at the piano, surrounded by flame, shards of glass, and smoke.

The Monster Ball

After plans for Lady Gaga's tour with Kanye West fell through, she immediately began preparing for a new tour, the Monster Ball. The

In November 2009, Lady Gaga bought $1,000 in pizza for fans who had spent the night lined up at a record store in Los Angeles to see her for an autograph signing.

new tour kicked off in Montreal, Canada, on November 27. Lady Gaga described the show as a pop opera. Just as with the Fame Ball, the Monster Ball featured elaborate staging and highly choreographed dance numbers. The show told the story of Lady Gaga's experience on the Fame Ball Tour, including the monsters she faced as a result of her fame. As the show progressed, Lady Gaga portrayed herself maturing emotionally as she overcomes the obstacles associated with fame.

"The theatrics and story elements are in the style of an opera," Lady Gaga told *Rolling Stone*. "Imagine if you could take the sets of an

Showy: Lady Gaga performs on January 20, 2010, in New York City during her Monster Ball Tour. She described the show as a pop opera.

opera, which are very grand and very beautiful, and put them through a pop-electro lens. The design of the show is very, very forward, very, very innovative. I've been thinking about ways to play with the shape of this stage and change the way that we watch things."

According to theater critic Kelly Nestruck, the effort was largely successful. He wrote, "While The Monster Ball has nothing on the great operas or the golden age of musical theatre, Lady Gaga's 'electro-pop opera' is at least twice as entertaining and infinitely fresher than any stage musical written over the last decade."

Lady Gaga next grabbed headlines in December, when she was invited to perform for Britain's Queen Elizabeth II at the Royal Variety Performance in London, England. Lady Gaga wore a long red latex dress with a 20-foot (6-meter) red train, puffy red sleeves, and a red Elizabethan ruff around her neck. The dress was designed in the style of something Britain's Queen Elizabeth I (1533–1603) would have worn. For her performance, Lady Gaga played the piano and sang "Speechless," suspended on a black swing 30 feet (9 m) above the stage. After the show, she was introduced to the queen. Photographers snapped away as twenty-three-year-old Lady Gaga curtsied and shook

Royalty: Queen Elizabeth II *(left)* meets Lady Gaga after the Royal Variety Performance in London on December 7, 2009. Gaga wore a red latex dress for the event.

hands with the eighty-three-year-old queen, who appeared quite entertained by Lady Gaga.

By 2010 it seemed that Lady Gaga was everywhere. Journalist Barbara Walters named her one of the 10 Most Fascinating People of 2009, which included a television interview on *20/20*. Lady Gaga dressed in a conservative black Chanel suit for the interview, and the two discussed fame, art, sexuality, and media attention. Lady Gaga told Walters that her main goals were the pursuit of love and art and to be a liberating influence for her young fans everywhere. In January 2010, Lady Gaga also appeared on the *Oprah Winfrey Show*, where she discussed her rapid rise to fame, her unique fashion sense, and her day-to-day life. That same month, she performed four shows at New York City's legendary Radio City Music Hall, earning rave reviews for her performances.

Being Covered

Lady Gaga is a talented songwriter. For this reason, a wide variety of artists have covered, or done their own versions of, her songs. Covering another artist's songs is common in the music world. Doing a cover is usually a tribute to the original artist and songwriter. It gives an artist a chance to put a new spin on a popular song. For example, pop star Katy Perry has done covers of Lady Gaga's "Poker Face" and "Born This Way." The progressive rock band Thirty Seconds to Mars included a cover of "Bad Romance" on the deluxe edition of their album *This Is War*. Chris Daughtry of *American Idol* fame performed a stripped-down, acoustic version of "Poker Face." Others to sing Lady Gaga songs include Hayley Williams of the band Paramore, the Arctic Monkeys, and the band New Years Day.

The Grammys

Many Lady Gaga fans were eagerly anticipating the annual Grammy Awards, held in January at the Staples Center in Los Angeles. The Grammys are the music industry's highest honor, and the awards ceremony is, for many, the musical highlight of the year. Lady Gaga was nominated for five awards, including Album of the Year (for *The Fame*) and Song of the Year (for "Poker Face"). However, much to the chagrin of many of her fans, Lady Gaga was not up for the Best Newcomer award. According to Grammy rules, Gaga wasn't a newcomer because she'd emerged as a star in 2008. For her part, Lady Gaga said that the minor controversy over her eligibility didn't matter to her. On an appearance on *The Tonight Show with Jay Leno*, she explained, "I truthfully don't rely on that outside validation. My fans are my family now, and really what I care about is what they think."

Winner: Lady Gaga poses with her awards in the photo room at the 2010 Grammy Awards. She was nominated for five awards.

Lady Gaga had already won two Grammys before the ceremony even started (some of the lower-profile awards are given out at a ceremony held before the main, televised one). *The Fame* won the award for Best Electronic/Dance Album, while "Poker Face" earned honors in the Best Dance Recording category.

A major awards show such as the Grammys attracts a lot of media attention. A big focus on the show is on what the stars will be wearing,

particularly Lady Gaga. In fact, viewership for the awards ceremony was the highest it had been in years, and many gave the credit to Lady Gaga. People wanted to see what she'd wear and what she'd do. Lady Gaga didn't let her fans down. She wore five different outfits during the show, including the futuristic white dress and glitter-covered bodysuit in which she arrived for the show.

Lady Gaga opened the show with "Poker Face." She wore a skimpy sequin-covered green leotard and matching ankle boots. Then she was joined onstage by music legend Elton John. The two musicians, wearing matching silver sequin glasses, played facing pianos for a duet that blended "Speechless" with the Elton John classic "Your Song." Lady Gaga didn't win any awards that night, but she was pleased. "I couldn't have had a more magical night," she said. "It went exactly perfect."

Duet with a legend: Elton John *(left)* and Lady Gaga perform on facing pianos during the Grammy Awards on January 31, 2010. They performed one of Lady Gaga's songs and one of Elton John's songs.

Brrring!: Lady Gaga appears on a late-night television talk show in London in March 2010 to promote her new single "Telephone."

Kinda Busy

Lady Gaga didn't slow down a bit after her big night at the 2010 Grammys. A new single off *The Fame Monster* had just been released. "Telephone" represented Lady Gaga's feelings of being cut off from a normal life because of her fame. The song was another collaboration with Beyoncé. In the music video, Beyoncé breaks Lady Gaga out of jail and they become fugitives (people running from the police). To gain freedom from the pressures of their fame, the two characters commit a mass murder in a diner and agree to flee far, far away. Originally, Lady

Sorry I cannot hear you: Beyoncé appears in the music video for "Telephone," a song, on which she collaborated with Lady Gaga for the album *The Fame Monster*. The video premiered on March 11, 2010.

Gaga had written the song for Britney Spears, but Spears rejected it. Lady Gaga decided to use it for herself.

"Telephone" went on to become another Gaga success, reaching No. 3 on the Hot 100 and selling more than 7 million copies. The song would later be nominated for a Grammy in the Best Pop Collaboration with Vocals category.

Back on Tour

The first North American leg of Lady Gaga's Monster Ball Tour ended January 26. She took a month off from touring, but shortly after the Grammys, she was back on the road for the European leg. Because of the sudden cancellation of the Fame Kills Tour with Kanye West, Lady Gaga had been forced to plan the Monster Ball much more quickly than she would have liked. She used the month to give the show a makeover, fixing aspects she didn't like and making it more suitable for the large arenas at which she was being booked.

The European leg of the tour finally kicked off in Manchester, England, on February 18, 2010. From there, it took Lady Gaga to Australia (where she celebrated her twenty-fourth birthday), Japan, back to Europe, and then back again to North America. Ticket sales were so good that the tour was often extended. Lady Gaga toured almost nonstop throughout most of the year, with only a few short breaks of a week or two.

Meanwhile, the third and final single from *The Fame Monster*, "Alejandro," was released. The song reached No. 5 on the Hot 100 chart, making it Lady Gaga's seventh consecutive Top 10 hit.

The travel-heavy tour was beginning to take a toll on the star, however. Lady Gaga would often fly from Europe to New York and back in a day. All the while, she was busy writing songs for her next album. In May the stress of the heavy travel and workload seemed to catch up with her.

Back on the road: Lady Gaga arrives for the Brit Awards on February 16, 2010, in London, England. The event was held two days before she kicked off the European leg of her Monster Ball Tour.

Third single: Lady Gaga performs "Alejandro" live on the *Today* show in July 2010. She wears the same short blonde bob as in the "Alejandro" music video.

Musical Influence: The Beatles

Perhaps no band has had more influence on modern pop and rock music than the Beatles. Like countless other artists, Lady Gaga credits the legendary rock band with being one of her biggest inspirations.

The Beatles formed in Liverpool, England, in 1960. The original band included John Lennon, Paul McCartney, George Harrison, and drummer Pete Best. (Ringo Star replaced Best in 1962.) From the release of their first album (1963's *Please, Please Me*), the band enjoyed almost unrivaled popularity worldwide, including in the United States, where Beatlemania caused fans by the thousands to mob the band anywhere they went. From 1963 until the band's breakup in 1970, they released hit after hit, including "Yesterday," "Let It Be," "Hey Jude," "All You Need Is Love," and many more.

Rock-and-roll legends: The Beatles perform on February 9, 1964, on the *Ed Sullivan Show*. Lady Gaga was inspired by this band from Liverpool, England.

She was scheduled to perform at the Costume Institute Gala at New York's Metropolitan Museum of Art. It is one of the biggest fashion events of the year and was cochaired by Oprah Winfrey and *Vogue* editor-in-chief Anna Wintour. But for some reason, Lady Gaga uncharacteristically locked herself in her dressing room before the show and refused to come out to perform. Finally, Winfrey—known for her skills in communicating and empathizing with others—went in to speak to Lady Gaga. Whatever Winfrey said or did, it worked. Lady Gaga came out and, an hour late, gave her performance.

The Meat Dress

The tour continued through summer, returning in late June to the United States. Meanwhile, Lady Gaga reunited with ex-boyfriend Luc Carl. The two made their new relationship public in early July when they attended a New York Mets baseball game together. Within months rumors swirled that the couple was engaged—or even married already.

Relationship: Lady Gaga attends a New York Mets game with her boyfriend Luc Carl *(far left)* in 2010. The two have been in and out of a relationship for years, but this outing made their relationship public.

September 13, 2010

A monster night for Lady Gaga at VMAs

From the Pages of USA TODAY

Lady Gaga may have cemented her reign as the leading lady of modern music by taking home the video of the year award for "Bad Romance," but all eyes were on Kanye West and Taylor Swift at the MTV Video Music Awards on Sunday.

Swift, whose acceptance speech for best female video last year was infamously interrupted by West, sang "Innocent," her never-before-heard new single from her upcoming album, *Speak Now*. Suited up in bright red, West closed the show with a song that toasted people behaving badly, while three ballerinas danced sweetly on the sidelines.

Gaga, who set a record with 13 nominations, took home two awards on the pre-show: best dance music video for "Bad Romance" and best collaboration for "Telephone" featuring Beyoncé.

Reign: Lady Gaga arrives at the 2010 MTV Video Music Awards in an Alexander McQueen dress.

Gaga also won the first award at the ceremony, with "Bad Romance" taking the moonman trophy for best female video. "Tonight, little monsters, we're the cool kids at the party," said Gaga, referring to her nickname for her fans.

She also thanked "the gays," U.S. servicemen and late [deceased] designer Alexander McQueen, whose elaborate creation she was wearing. "Bad Romance" went on to win for best pop video.

When "Bad Romance" took the final and top award of the night, Gaga announced the name of her new record. "It's called *Born This Way*," said the eccentric singer, before breaking into song.

On the red carpet, everyone, it seemed, had one person on the brain. Said Akon, "I'm excited to see Lady Gaga take home all those awards."

—Cindy Clark

Lady Gaga never commented on it. While some have questioned whether Carl treats Lady Gaga with the respect she deserves, others have said that the renewed relationship gave her a much-needed boost.

She was about to get a big professional boost as well. In August MTV released the list of VMA nominees. Lady Gaga dominated the list with a record total of thirteen nominations, including two for Video of the Year ("Bad Romance" and "Telephone").

She didn't perform at the award ceremony on September 12. Yet Lady Gaga unquestionably stole the headlines that night—and not just because she won a record eight VMA awards, including Video of the Year, Best Female Video, and Best Pop Video (all for "Bad Romance"), as well as Best Pop Collaboration with Vocals (with Beyoncé, for "Telephone"). On this night, it was Lady Gaga's fashion sense that made the news. As she usually does for award ceremonies, Lady Gaga showed up with several changes of outfits. The outfit everyone was talking about afterward was the one she wore as she accepted the award for Video of the Year: a dress made of raw meat, complete with a meat hat, shoes, and a purse.

The dress, created by designer Franc Fernandez, drew a wide range of reactions. Some who knew Lady Gaga well weren't surprised. She'd done a photo shoot earlier that year for a Japanese magazine wearing a bikini made of meat. Others were shocked or offended. Many in the audience didn't even really believe that the dress was made entirely of raw meat.

Lady Gaga wasn't just trying to shock people for no reason. The meat dress came with a message. She arrived at the ceremony with four former soldiers who had been discharged (released) from the U.S. military because of its "don't ask, don't tell" policy. From 1993 until 2010, this policy allowed gays to serve in the military as long as they were not open about their homosexuality. As a gay rights activist, Lady Gaga was protesting this rule (the repeal of which is pending appeal) and the meat dress was how she sent the message.

"What I was really trying to say was dead meat is dead meat," Lady Gaga later explained. "And anyone that's willing to take their life and die for their country is the same. You're not gay and dead, straight and dead. You are dead."

Not all viewers responded positively. The animal rights organization People for the Ethical Treatment of Animals (PETA) was among the many groups to protest. PETA issued a statement saying, "No matter how beautifully it is presented, flesh from a tortured animal is flesh from a tortured animal. Meat represents bloody violence and suffering, so if that's the look they were going for, they achieved it."

"It is certainly no disrespect to anyone that is vegan or vegetarian," Lady Gaga responded. "However . . . if we don't stand up for what we believe in and if we don't fight for our rights, pretty soon we're going to have as much rights as the meat on our own bones. And I am not a piece of meat."

Flesh: Lady Gaga accepts the award for Video of the Year while wearing her famous meat dress during the MTV Video Music Awards on September 12, 2010. The entire outfit was made of raw meat—even her hat, shoes, and purse.

October 6, 2010

Halloween's 'It Girl' this year by far: Lady Gaga

From the Pages of USA TODAY

Don't be shocked if Lady Gaga—make that lots of Lady Gagas—show up at your Halloween party.

A slew of Lady Gaga costumes and accessories targeted at teens and adults are turning the $3.5 billion costume industry on its head this Halloween.

It's the first time in memory that the hottest holiday costume isn't one for the kid market—but for adults. "As a personality, Lady Gaga is the single most popular costume we've sold for adults in our 59 years in business," says Howard Beige, executive vice president of Rubie's Costume Co.

Rubie's has the license to make Lady Gaga costumes and accessories, such as big blond wigs, extra large sunglasses and even Lady Gaga makeup. It expects to sell at least 1 million Lady Gaga items by Halloween. That eclipses the tally for the Michael Jackson items it heavily sold last year.

The popularity of the Lady Gaga costumes signals the changing nature of Halloween—which has increasingly become a party holiday for adults. What's more, Lady Gaga costumes come with a crucial touch of reality: She's actually worn similar outfits.

"She is Halloween," says Robert Thompson, professor of pop culture at Syracuse University. "It's too easy to be Lady Gaga. All you need to do is put on a bunch of feathers and other stuff that sticks out. It seems so lazy."

Among the hot Gaga items:

- Costumes. The Lady Gaga 2009 Video Music Awards performance outfit—white shorts and high white boots—goes for $49 to $59, as does the ultra-low-cut Lady Gaga blue swimsuit and the outer-space-like Lady Gaga black-and-silver dress.

But don't look for the controversial raw meat dress that Lady Gaga wore to the 2010 Video Music Awards. "We'll leave that for consumers to create on their own," says Rubie's Beige.

- Wigs. An array of Lady Gaga blond wigs—and blond hair bow—go for $14.98 to $19.98.
- Sunglasses. Mask-like sunglasses, including one that says "Gaga" on it in large letters, fetch up to $9.98.
- Makeup. Lady Gaga makeup kits—with five colored makeup sticks—sell for $5.99 to $7.99.

"We have a waiting list for Lady Gaga costumes that's through the roof," says Travis Mattick, marketing manager at Halloweencostumes.com.

BuyCostumes.com bought every Lady Gaga item it could, says merchandising VP Sean Clark.

Some folks are trying to do Lady Gaga on a budget by just buying big blond wigs and large sunglasses, says Brad Butler, COO at HalloweenExpress.com.

Because of such intense interest in Lady Gaga, says Beige, Rubie's already is planning slightly less racy Gaga wear for next Halloween that can be targeted to the lucrative pre-teen set.

—Bruce Horovitz

Boo!: Lady Gaga was the leading costume for adults in 2010. This was one of the costumes people could buy to look like the star.

Back to Work

Lady Gaga didn't have much time to dwell on the controversy. Two nights later, she was back on tour, performing in Philadelphia, Pennsylvania. And less than a month after that, she was on a flight bound for Finland to begin yet another European leg of the tour. She won three more MTV Europe Music Awards on November 7, which she accepted via satellite during a show in Budapest, Hungary. She continued touring Europe through December 21, when she finally returned home for an extended break.

IN FOCUS

Graphic Imagery

When Lady Gaga makes a video, she doesn't pull any punches. Her videos are known for portraying graphic violence and sexuality, as well as for addressing a wide variety of taboos.

Videos such as "Paparazzi," "Bad Romance," and "Telephone" have focused on themes of violence, murder, and suicide. Most of Gaga's videos also explore graphic sexuality, in all its forms—straight, gay, interracial, and more. Other controversial subject matter has included religion, the occult (supernatural, magical powers, often of a dark nature), and even the Nazi soldiers and imagery of the video for "Alejandro."

For many fans, this is part of Gaga's appeal. They see her freedom to express herself without regard for societal norms as an inspiration. Fans admire her for sending a message of taking control of one's own life and confronting its challenges on the individual's own terms. For other viewers, Lady Gaga's video imagery is deeply disturbing, offering a dark, grisly, and tortured view of humanity. For example, the "Telephone" video was considered to be so explicit and oriented so much to adult content that MTV almost banned it. Yet, many in the music industry admire the video for its unflinching artistry. That means Gaga has created a media sensation that keeps people talking.

In 2010 Lady Gaga became the first artist to get more than 1 billion video hits on the popular media site YouTube.

While Lady Gaga was taking a couple of months off from touring, that didn't mean that she wasn't hard at work. She and Elton John recorded a duet of the song "Hello, Hello" for the animated film *Gnomeo and Juliet* (2011). She was also putting the finishing touches on her next album, to be titled *Born This Way*. On January 1, 2011, Lady Gaga posted on her Twitter account that the first single, also called "Born This Way," would be released in February. The album, meanwhile, was scheduled for a May 2011 release.

USA TODAY Snapshots®

Tuning in to YouTube

Among U.S. adults who have ever watched a video on YouTube, 42% say they use the site frequently, up from 33% in 2006. Weekly use among YouTube viewers:

	More than 2 hours	1-2 hours	Less than 1 hour	Only visited once or a few times
2006	2%	7%	24%	67%
2007	2%	10%	30%	58%

Source: Harris Poll online survey of 2,455 U.S. adults, including 1,587 YouTube viewers, conducted Nov. 7-13.

By Cindy Clark and Alejandro Gonzalez, USA TODAY, 2008

Vessel: Lady Gaga emerges from an egg while performing onstage at the 2011 Grammy Awards. She arrived at the awards carried in the egg.

Born This *Way* and Beyond

Lady Gaga wasn't shy about building up expectations for her third album, *Born This Way*. "I promise you, I'll never let you down," she told her fans. "The album's finished and it's . . . really good. . . . I promise to give you the greatest album of this decade, just for you."

In a later interview, she tried to describe the sound of the album. She called it "a marriage of electronic music

with . . . metal or rock 'n' roll, pop, anthemic [rousing or uplifting] style melodies with really sledge-hammering dance beats."

A New Sound?

The first chance many fans got to hear Lady Gaga's new sound was at the Grammy Awards in Los Angeles on February 13, 2011. Lady Gaga showed up at the award ceremony encased inside a huge egg, which she called a vessel. She didn't walk the red carpet but was carried inside the egg into the auditorium. She later told an interviewer that she had spent three straight days inside the egg and that it was a great creative experience.

Finally, as the show opened, the egg was carried onstage, the music started, and Lady Gaga hatched. She gave a highly choreographed and enthusiastic performance of "Born This Way," complete with a smoking piano covered with plastic heads, dancers stripping down to their underwear, and lots and lots of latex. On the awards side of

The video: Lady Gaga appears in the music video for the song "Born This Way." The video was nominated in the new category Best Video with a Message at the 2011 MTV Video Music Awards.

As part of the promotion of *Born This Way*, *Vogue* fashion magazine featured Lady Gaga on the cover of its March 2011 issue. For the cover shoot, Lady Gaga wore a simple, elegant, low-cut cream-colored dress and a hot-pink wig. Her makeup was equally simple, featuring pale blonde eyebrows and maroon lipstick.

the show, it was a good night. Lady Gaga won three times—*The Fame Monster* for Pop Vocal Album and "Bad Romance" for Female Pop Vocal Performance and for Best Short Form Music Video.

The reaction to "Born This Way" was mixed. Many of Lady Gaga's hardcore fans loved it. It brought a highly danceable beat, and its lyrics conveyed a positive, uplifting message of self-acceptance. *Billboard's* Jem Aswad wrote, "If fans were looking for something big, anthemic, positive and global, they weren't the least bit disappointed. 'Born This Way' is massive in every way: It's a huge-sounding single with a pulsating beat and a love-yourself message that's bound to pack dance floors and blast from cars, computers and radios for weeks to come." Most music fans agreed, and the single debuted at No. 1 on the Hot 100—the first Lady Gaga

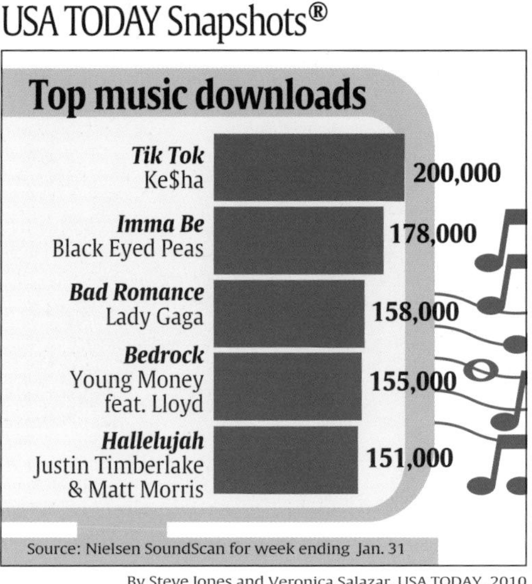

By Steve Jones and Veronica Salazar, USA TODAY, 2010

song to debut at the top.

The praise was far from unanimous, however. Lady Gaga prided herself on being original and one-of-a-kind. But many fans, critics, and even fellow musicians were critical of the song. They said it was a direct rip-off of Madonna's 1989 hit "Express Yourself." Furthermore, Lady Gaga's dance moves at the Grammy Awards were evocative of Madonna's famous moves in her "Vogue" video. Some observers even remarked that Lady Gaga dressed and *looked* like Madonna at the awards ceremony.

"The problem with the song is not just that it's hard to escape the feeling we've heard it before," wrote the *Telegraph*'s Neil McCormick, "but that it's too easy to pin point exactly where we've heard it before.

Compared: Some people thought Lady Gaga *(right)* looked like Madonna when Gaga attended the Grammy Awards in February 2011. Madonna *(left)* is pictured in 1999 with a tall ponytail, leotards, and a cone bra on her Blonde Ambition World Tour.

Drama: In February 2011, Lady Gaga went on *The Tonight Show with Jay Leno* and talked about *Born This Way* being compared to Madonna's earlier work.

Basically it is a reworking of Madonna's "Express Yourself" with a touch of Madonna's "Vogue." Which is a bit too much Madonna for someone who is trying to establish her own identity as the, er, new Madonna."

As the debate over the song grew, Lady Gaga made an appearance on *The Tonight Show with Jay Leno*. Leno asked her about the comparison. Lady Gaga answered, "The good news is that I got an email from her [Madonna's] people and her, sending me their love and complete support on behalf of the single, and if the queen says it shall be, then

Lady Gaga had a deal with the retail chain Target to distribute a special edition of *Born This Way*. But in March 2011, she backed out of the deal. She said she did so because Target had in the past supported political candidates who fought against gay rights.

Duet: Ten-year-old Maria Aragon performs "Born This Way" on stage with Lady Gaga at a concert in Toronto, Canada, on March 3, 2011.

it shall be." But then, things got even stranger. Madonna's publicist said that no such e-mail had been sent. Had Lady Gaga made it up? Stories sprang up all over the Internet calling Gaga a liar.

Regardless of the drama, "Born This Way" had quickly become a huge hit. Soon YouTube was flooded with amateur covers of the song. One, in particular, went viral (suddenly grew very popular). Ten-year-old Canadian Maria Aragon's stripped-down piano version of the song got millions of hits. Lady Gaga—already back on tour—saw the video and was so touched by it that it moved her to tears. Lady Gaga surprised Maria by inviting her to perform the song together at a concert in Toronto, Canada, on March 3. Aragon sat on Lady Gaga's lap at a piano, and they sang a duet of Aragon's version of the song. The gesture was representative of the close relationship the star feels with her many fans, whom she lovingly calls her little monsters.

Smash Hit

The album *Born This Way*, released May 23, 2011, was an instant hit. More than one million copies of the album sold within the first week—for only the seventeenth time in the history of the Billboard charts. The album's sales were driven in part by a one-day Amazon.com

June 2, 2011

Gaga's *Born* Delivers Record Sales

From the Pages of USA TODAY

A string of hit records and a massive marketing campaign boosted Lady Gaga's *Born This Way* to the biggest first-week album sales in six years, a strategic success that industry observers say won't be easily replicated.

The 1.11 million copies she sold, the most since 50 Cent's *The Massacre* sold 1.14 million in 2005, is the result of a steady stream of TV appearances including recent ones on *Saturday Night Live, American Idol* and *Good Morning America*, buzzworthy videos, a rabid fan base and widespread availability. Taylor Swift, whose *Speak Now* sold 1 million when it was released in November, was the last album to hit the mark.

"Whenever an album sells so much in one week, people ask if it's an indication of something broader," says Keith Caulfield, *Billboard*'s associate director of charts/retail. "She is a true pop superstar, ostensibly the biggest in the past three years. Every single is a hit. Every video is a water-cooler moment. All eyes are on Gaga."

The album's sales were helped when Amazon, which often offers $2.99 daily deals on new and hit albums, decided to make *Born This Way* available for 99 cents. Albums wholesale for more than $8 and sell for an average of $11.99, according to *Billboard*. The response to the Amazon sale was so massive that the retailer's servers slowed.

"We saw extraordinary response far above what we expected," says Amazon spokeswoman Cat Griffin. "We've never seen this much interest in one album in such a short period."

deal that offered a virtually unheard-of price of 99 cents. (Amazon was willing to take a loss on the album sales to publicize its new music service, a competitor of the industry giant iTunes, which listed the album for $11.99). The response was so heavy that the Amazon servers couldn't keep up with demand, causing long delays for customers. However, the Amazon deal also sparked controversy in the music in-

Gaga's first-week sales are "exciting, but an anomaly [unusual event]," says Alicia Dennis, music editor for interactive pop-culture magazine Zimbio.com. "Amazon's promotion was a great way to catch people who might have turned to other means (like cloud systems or illegal downloads) to listen to the new album.

"This kind of promotion could definitely boost sales for other artists, but they'd have to have Lady Gaga's hype working for them as well, and no one does hype like Lady Gaga."

Ean Mering of Pomegranate, a digital media network agency that provides brand development for artists and music companies, says a low-price strategy could have future benefits.

"This pricing approach will prove to be a great case study," Mering says, adding:

"This is a good move that could open up Gaga to audiences who would not previously have purchased a $7.99 record."

—Steve Jones

Sales: Lady Gaga appears at a store in New York City to sign copies of her album *Born This Way* in May 2011.

dustry. Some complained that such deals deflated the price of all music, which would in turn hurt record companies and artists.

Critical reception for the album was mostly favorable. Rob Sheffield of *Rolling Stone* heaped praise on Gaga for her honestly and boldness. "What makes *Born This Way* so disarmingly great is how warm and humane Gaga sounds," he wrote. "There isn't a subtle moment on

May 23, 2011

Lady Gaga, truly 'Born' to be fame's mistress

From the Pages of USA TODAY

Even Lady Gaga's most ardent admirers would have trouble contesting this point: The woman who just replaced Oprah as *Forbes*' most powerful celebrity is more famous for her voracity [hunger for] and canniness in chasing fame and clinging to it than she is for any singular talent or accomplishment.

That might not be a problem if Gaga were a Real Housewife, a C-list *Dancing With the Stars* contestant or any number of aggressively unexceptional media hounds who have somehow managed to captivate the public in recent years. But for an artist who has achieved her level of prominence and clearly cares about old-school virtues such as respect and staying power, it's a precarious position.

On Gaga's new album, *Born This Way* (1/2 out of four), out today, it's not always easy to distinguish between her creative ambition and her desire to simply sustain and milk our fascination.

This has been true of other pop icons, notably Madonna, whom Gaga apes

the album, but even at its nuttiest, the music is full of wide-awake emotional details." But not everyone agreed. Chris Richards of the *Washington Post* described the album as boring. "[It] feels conservative and predictable," he continued. "And at its worst, it sounds like reheated leftovers from some '80s movie soundtrack."

Of course, Gaga didn't pull any punches on the new album, which left her once again at the center of a controversy. Some claimed that the album's second single and video, "Judas," was anti-Christian. In the song, Gaga sings of being torn between Jesus and Judas (the man who betrays Jesus in the Bible), and professes her love for Judas. These

Born This Way and Beyond · **95**

shamelessly on the first single and title track. But at this stage in her career, Madonna's singles had a freshness and genuine yearning that defied attempts to cast her as [merely provocative].

Gaga's new tunes seem cooler and more calculated, sucking you in (or banging you over the head) with a barrage of bracing grooves that can grow numbing. There's the pummeling electronica of "Judas," the breathless Eurodisco of "Scheibe," the winking, Latin-tinged dance-pop of "Americano."

Other songs embrace more classic and conservative textures, evoking radio hits from and before the 25-year-old singer/songwriter's preschool years.

In fact, the most daring aspect of *Born This Way* may be its unabashed nostalgia. A number of tracks are heavily influenced by '80s rock. E Street Band sax player Clarence Clemons is a guest, and you could easily imagine the power ballad "You And I", with its soaring vocals and bombastic guitar riffs (by Queen's Brian May), being played in an arena as the audience waves lighters in unison.

Gaga's platform, too, is at its core a traditional one for a pop star. Let your freak flag fly, she tells fans, and let everyone else do the same. There are numerous references to New Testament figures (and here's to you again, Ms. Ciccone) and a bit of quasi-social commentary. Predictably, Gaga fares best when she keeps her observations general and peppers them with wry humor.

"I'm a disaster . . . just a freedom hussy," she sings on the buzzy, bubbly "Bad Kids," adding, "I will survive." Time will tell whether Gaga protests too much, but *Born This Way*, for all its shortcomings, should ensure that we don't forget her anytime soon.

—Elysa Gardner

lyrics even prompted the nation of Lebanon to ban the album. For her part, Gaga dismissed the controversy, saying that Judas is merely a metaphor for a boyfriend who betrayed her.

The Future

Lady Gaga has burst onto the worldwide entertainment scene as few others have done before. In just a couple of years, she went from a virtual unknown to a pop megastar. In fact, in May 2011, *Forbes* magazine released its Celebrity 100 list of the most powerful people in entertainment. *Forbes* gave Lady Gaga the top spot, citing her estimated

Musical Influence: Pink Floyd

One of the bands Lady Gaga used to cover back in her days as a rocker was Pink Floyd. The British band's often deep, philosophical sound resonated with young Stefani. Pink Floyd formed in 1965 and was an underground hit in London in the late 1960s. The original lineup included Syd Barrett, Roger Waters, Richard Wright, and Nick Mason, though membership shifted quite a bit over the band's decades of success. Pink Floyd was known for having deep, philosophical lyrics and an experimental sound. From 1967 to 1994, the band released fourteen albums. The most widely known of these were probably 1973's *The Dark Side of the Moon* and 1979's *The Wall*, both of which reached No. 1 in the United States.

earings of $90 million, her 32 million Facebook friends, and her 10 million Twitter followers. Oprah Winfrey came in second, followed by pop star Justin Bieber. Lady Gaga's natural talent, dynamic style, and savvy marketing sense have turned her into a household name.

Unlike many overnight pop sensations, Lady Gaga seems to have staying power. She writes almost all of her own music and lyrics, and behind all the publicity stunts and wild outfits, she's got the voice to back it all up. And there's likely not a harder worker in the business. Lady Gaga is almost constantly working. Few artists could keep up the grueling tour schedule she's maintained since 2009. In an industry where an artist often requires three or four years to complete an album, Lady Gaga has finished three best sellers in as many years, with almost all the work being done on the road. Her unique sound and style have changed the face of pop music, from inspiring the way stars dress to igniting a renewed interest in political activism. Of course, she's also inspired more than a few imitators. But no imitator can come close to the real thing. Lady Gaga is one of a kind.

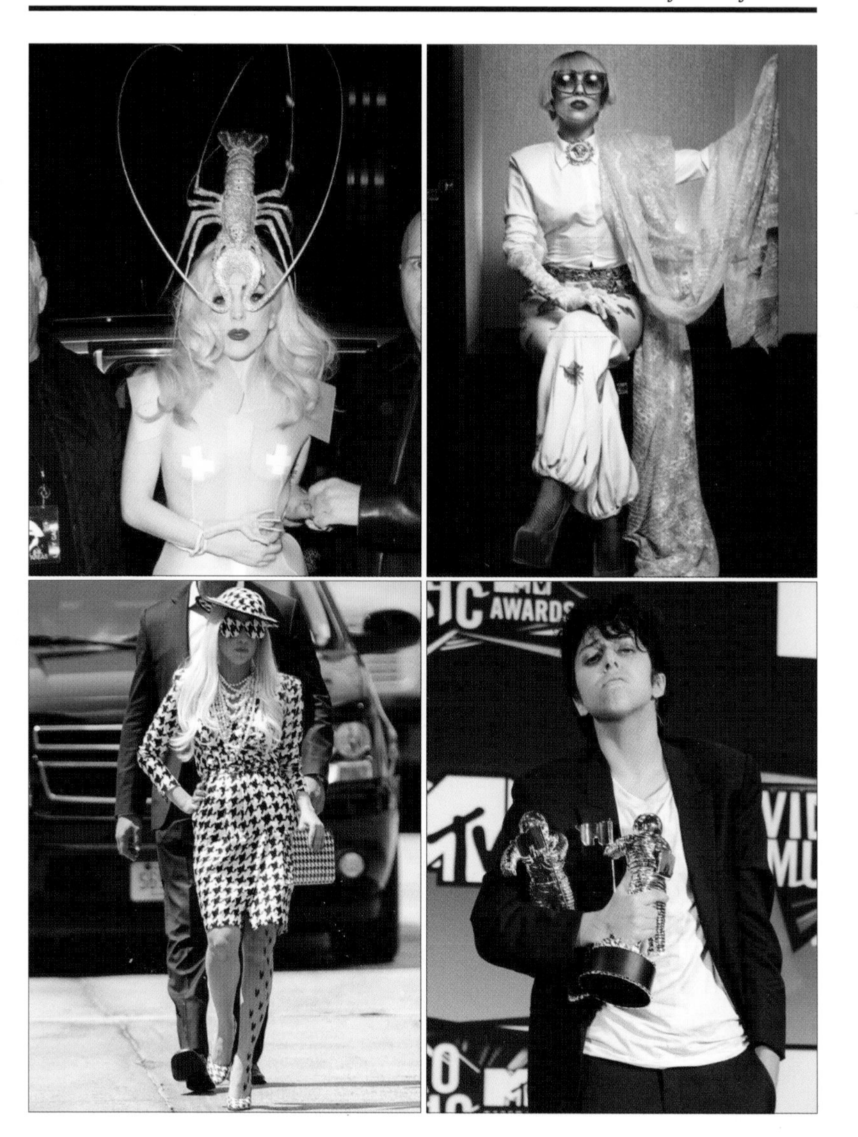

The looks: Lady Gaga is known for her style and for pushing gender boundaries. *Clockwise from top left*: She wears a see-through outfit, silver lobster hat, and a chicken claw on her wrist in February 2010. She wears short green hair and bright red shoes at the Four Seasons Hotel in Sydney, Australia, in July 2011. She holds her awards while dressed as Jo Calderone (her fictional male model personality) at the MTV Video Music Awards in August 2011. She leaves a taping of the *View* in New York City in August 2011 in head-to-toe houndstooth.

TIMELINE

1986 Stefani Joanne Angelina Germanotta is born in New York City on March 28.

1990 Stefani begins taking piano lessons.

1997 Stefani attends the private all-girls school Convent of the Sacred Heart.

2004 Stefani gains early admittance to New York University's Tisch School of the Arts.

2005 Stefani leaves school and moves into an apartment on Manhattan's Lower East Side. She takes an internship with music producer Irwin Robinson.

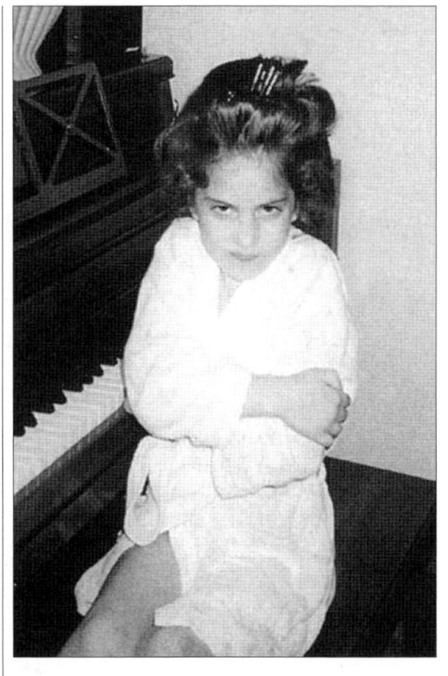

Piano girl: Stefani didn't enjoy piano lessons as a young girl in New York City.

2006 Producer Rob Fusari signs Stefani to a management contract. She builds a new look, style, and sound and takes the stage name Lady Gaga. She signs a recording deal with Island Def Jam.

2007 Island Def Jam drops Lady Gaga. She signs with Interscope. In August she performs at the Lollapalooza music festival in Chicago, Illinois. Late in the year, she moves to Los Angeles, California.

2008 Lady Gaga's first single, "Just Dance," is released in April.

Lady Gaga's debut album, *The Fame*, is released in August.

In September Lady Gaga tours with the New Kids on the Block. "Poker Face" is released as a single.

Controversy erupts in November after Christina Aguilera is accused of copying Lady Gaga's style.

2009 Lady Gaga opens for the Pussycat Dolls in January in Europe.

The Fame Ball Tour begins in March.

Lady Gaga performs at the Glastonbury Festival of Contemporary Performing Arts in Somerset, England, in June.

Lady Gaga shocks the audience in September at the MTV Video Music Awards with her mock suicide by hanging during a performance of "Paparazzi."

Lady Gaga speaks on behalf of gay rights in Washington, D.C., at the Human Rights Campaign National Dinner and at the National Equality March in October.

The Fame Monster is released in November. Lady Gaga appears on *Saturday Night Live* and at the American Music Awards. The Monster Ball Tour begins.

In December Lady Gaga performs at the Royal Variety Performance in London, England, before Queen Elizabeth II.

Living large: Lady Gaga performs high in the air on a tall piano wearing a long red latex dress at the Royal Variety Performance in London, England, in December 2009.

2010 Lady Gaga performs with Elton John at the Grammys in January.

Lady Gaga reunites with ex-boyfriend Luc Carl in June. The couple splits later that year.

In September Lady Gaga wins a record eight Video Music Awards. She makes headlines by wearing an outfit made entirely of raw meat.

2011 Lady Gaga releases the song "Born This Way" and performs it at the Grammys in February. She comes under heavy criticism for appearing to have copied Madonna's sound.

Lady Gaga performs onstage in March with ten-year-old Canadian fan Maria Aragon in an acoustic version of "Born This Way."

Lady Gaga's third album, *Born This Way*, is released in May. Sales top one million within a week. Online retailer Amazon.com creates a controversy by selling digital copies of the album for ninety-nine cents in a special one-day promotion.

Lady Gaga makes headlines by showing up for the Video Music Awards dressed as a man. She calls her male alter ego Joe Calderone.

DISCOGRAPHY

The Fame
Label: Interscope
Released: August 19, 2008

The Fame Monster
Label: Interscope
Released: November 18, 2009

Born This Way
Label: Interscope
Released: May 23, 2011

SOURCE NOTES

7 Jocelyn Vena, "Lady Gaga's Shocking 2009 VMA Fashion Choices," *MTV.com*, September 14, 2009, http://www.mtv.com/news/articles/1621407/lady-gagas-shocking-2009-vma-fashion-choices.jhtml (July 15, 2011).

7 Maureen Callahan, *Poker Face: The Rise and Rise of Lady Gaga* (New York: Hyperion, 2010), 197.

9 Emily Herbert. *Lady Gaga: Behind the Fame* (New York: Overlook Press, 2010), 11.

10 Vanessa Grigoriadis, "Growing Up Gaga." *New York Magazine*, March 28, 2010, http://nymag.com/arts/popmusic/features/65127/index2.html (July 15, 2011).

10 Herbert, *Lady Gaga: Behind the Fame*, 194.

10 Ibid.

11 Callahan, *Poker Face*, 15.

12 Herbert, *Lady Gaga: Behind the Fame*, 25.

13 Ibid., 13–14.

14 Grigoriadis, "Growing Up Gaga."

15 Callahan, *Poker Face*, 20.

15 Ibid., 23.

18 Ibid., 36.

19 Maureen Callahan and Sara Stewart, "Who's That Lady?" *New York Post*, January 21, 2010, http://www.nypost.com/p/entertainment/music/who_that_lady_CBlHI927dRlLmIwjVfGrwK/1 (July 15, 2011).

19 Annette Witheridge, "'I Made Lady Gaga': The Girl Who Changed Stefani Germanotta's Life with a Phone Call," *Mirror*, March 13, 2010, http://www.mirror.co.uk/celebs/news/2010/03/13/i-made-lady-gaga-the-girl-who-changed-stefani-germanotta-s-life-with-a-phone-call-115875-22107298/ (July 15, 2011).

19 Ibid.

20 Ibid.

25 Callahan, *Poker Face*, 55.

25 Ibid., 69.

30 Herbert, *Lady Gaga: Behind the Fame*, 123–124.

30 Callahan, *Poker Face*, 100.

33 Matt Thomas, "Going Gaga," *Fab*, n.d., http://www

.fabmagazine.com/features/362/Gaga.html (July 15, 2011).

36 Herbert, *Lady Gaga: Behind the Fame*, 60.

37 Callahan, *Poker Face*, 110.

39 Herbert, *Lady Gaga: Behind the Fame*, 72–73.

41 Ibid., 110.

47 Kerri Mason, "The Fame," *Billboard.com*, November 1, 2008, http://www.billboard.com/news/the-fame-1003877581.story#/news/the-fame-1003877581.story (July 15, 2011).

47 Alexis Petridis, "Lady Gaga, *The Fame*," *Guardian*, January 9, 2009, http://www.guardian.co.uk/music/2009/jan/09/lady-gaga-the-fame (July 15, 2011).

47 Ibid.

47 Jamie Gill, "Lady Gaga: *The Fame*," Yahoo! Music, January 15, 2009, http://uk.launch.yahoo.com/090115/33/220fu.html (July 15, 2011).

50 Chris Williams, "Lady Gaga: *Poker Face*," *Billboard*, February 28, 2009, 35.

51 *Daily Mail*, "Christina Aguilera Copies Lady Gaga as She Dons PVC Outfit in New Video," April 27, 2010, http://www.dailymail.co.uk/tvshowbiz/article-1269136/Christina-Aguilera-copies-Lady-GaGa-dons-PVC-outfit-new-video.html (July 15, 2011).

53 Herbert, *Lady Gaga: Behind the Fame*, 89.

54 Callahan, *Poker Face*, 179–180.

55 James Montgomery, "Lady Gaga Promises 'Life-Changing Experience' with Fame Ball Tour," *MTV.com*, February 4, 2009, http://www.mtv.com/news/articles/1604302/lady-gaga-launches-fame-ball-tour.jhtml (July 15, 2011).

56 Herbert, *Lady Gaga: Behind the Fame*, 145.

59 Christopher Muther, "Lady Gaga Shines in Song and Spectacle," *Boston Globe*, April 2, 2009, http://www.boston.com/ae/music/articles/2009/04/02/lady_gaga_shines_in_song_and_spectacle (July 15, 2011).

59 Whitney Pastorek, "Lady Gaga Live in L.A.," *Entertainment Weekly*, March 14, 2009, http://popwatch.ew.com/2009/03/14/lady-gaga-live (July 15, 2011).

59 Petridis, "Lady Gaga: *The Fame*."

62 Ibid., 204.

64 Ibid., 209.

65 Edna Gundersen, "Lady Gaga's Ice-Hearted 'Monster,'" *USA Today*, November 24, 2009.

66 Jem Aswad, "Madonna Says She's 'Very Flattered' by Lady Gaga Comparisons," *MTV.com*, September 14, 2009, http://www.mtv.com/news/articles/1621452/madonna-shes-very-flattered-by-lady-gaga-comparisons.jhtml (July 15, 2011).

70 Kelly Nestruck, "Lady Gaga's Monster Ball, Reviewed by a Theatre Critic," *Guardian*, November 30, 2009, http://www.guardian.co.uk/music/musicblog/2009/nov/30/lady-gaga-monster-ball (July 15, 2011).

72 James Dinh, "Lady Gaga Brings S&M 'Bad Romance' to 'Jay Leno Show,'" *MTV.com*, November 24, 2009, http://www.mtv.com/news/articles/1626952/lady-gaga-brings-sm-bad-romance-jay-leno-show.jhtml (July 15, 2011).

73 Donna Freydkin, "Lady Gaga Makes AIDS Awareness Her Cause," *USA Today*, February 15, 2010.

81 CBS, "Lady Gaga's Meat Dress: Outfit with a Message?" *CBS.com*, February 13, 2011, http://www.cbsnews.com/stories/2011/02/13/60minutes/main20031711.shtml (July 15, 2011).

81 Jocelyn Vena, "Lady Gaga's Meat Dress Draws Criticism from PETA," *MTV.com*, September 13, 2010, http://www.mtv.com/news/articles/1647732/lady-gaga-meat-dress-draws-criticism-from-peta.jhtml (July 15, 2011).

81 Ibid.

86 James Dinh, "Lady Gaga Says *Born This Way* Will Be 'Greatest Album of This Decade,'" *MTV.com*, November 29, 2010, http://www.mtv.com/news/articles/1653141/lady-gaga-born-this-way-will-be-greatest-album-this-decade.jhtml (July 15, 2011).

87 Greg Cochrane, "Lady Gaga Reveals Plans for *Born This Way* album," BBC, December 20, 2010, http://www.bbc.co.uk/newsbeat/12038773 (July 15, 2011).

88 Jem Aswad, "Single Review: Lady Gaga 'Born This Way,'" *Billboard.com*, February 11, 2011, http://www.billboard.com/news/single-review-lady-gaga-born-this-way-1005032432.story#/news/single-review-lady-gaga-born-this-way-1005032432.story (July 15, 2011).

90 Neil McCormick, "Lady Gaga: Is *Born This Way* the "Gayest Song 'Ever'?" *Telegraph*, February 11, 2011, http://blogs.telegraph.co.uk/culture/neilmccormick/100051388/

lady-gaga-is-born-this-way-the-gayest-song-ever (July 15, 2011).

91 Gil Kaufman, "Lady Gaga Says Madonna Approves Of 'Born This Way,'" *MTV.com*, February 15, 2011, http://www.mtv.com/news/articles/1657997/lady-gaga-madonna-leno.jhtml (July 15, 2011).

94 Rob Scheffield, "Lady Gaga: *Born This Way*," *RollingStone.com*, May 20, 2011, http://www.rollingstone.com/music/albumreviews/born-this-way-20110520 (July 15, 2011).

94 Chris Richards, "Lady Gaga's 'Born This Way': Music Is Preaching to the Bored Choir," *WashingtonPost.com*, May 20, 2011, http://www.washingtonpost.com/lifestyle/style/lady-gagas-born-this-way-music-is-preaching-to-the-bored-choir/2011/05/20/AFmiK27G_story.html (July 15, 2011).

SELECTED BIBLIOGRAPHY

Aswad, Jem. "Single Review: Lady Gaga, 'Born This Way.'" *Billboard.com*, February 11, 2011. http://www.billboard.com/news/single-review-lady-gaga-born-this-way-1005032432.story#/news/single-review-lady-gaga-born-this-way-1005032432.story (July 18, 2011).

Callahan, Maureen. *Poker Face: The Rise and Rise of Lady Gaga*. New York: Hyperion, 2010.

Callahan, Maureen, and Sara Stewart. "Who's That Lady?" *New York Post*, January 21, 2010. http://www.nypost.com/p/entertainment/music/who_that_lady_CBlHI927dRlLmIwjVfGrwK/0 (July 18, 2011).

Grigoriadis, Vanessa. "Growing Up Gaga." *New York Magazine*, March 28, 2010. http://nymag.com/arts/popmusic/features/65127/index2.html (July 15, 2011).

Herbert, Emily. *Lady Gaga: Behind the Fame*. New York: Overlook Press, 2010.

Lady Gaga: One Sequin at a Time. DVD. Directed by Sonia Anderson. Needham, MA: Echo Bridge Home Entertainment, 2010.

Scheffield, Rob. "Lady Gaga: *Born This Way*." *Rolling Stone.com*, May 20, 2011. http://www.rollingstone.com/music/albumreviews/born-this-way-20110520 (July 18, 2011).

Vena, Jocelyn. "Lady Gaga's Meat Dress Draws Criticism from PETA." *MTV.com*. September 13, 2010. http://www.mtv.com/news/articles/1647732/lady-gaga-meat-dress-draws-criticism-from-peta.jhtml (July 18, 2011).

Witheridge, Annette. "'I Made Lady GaGa': The Girl Who Changed Stefani Germanotta's Life with a Phone Call." *Mirror*, March 13, 2010. http://www.mirror.co.uk/celebs/news/2010/03/13/i-made-lady-gaga-the-girl-who-changed-stefani-germanotta-s-life-with-a-phone-call-115875-22107298/ (July 18, 2011).

FURTHER READING AND WEBSITES

Books

Andryszewski, Tricia. *Same-Sex Marriage: Granting Equal Rights or Damaging the Status of Marriage?* Minneapolis: Twenty-First Century Books, 2012.

Boaz, Claire Kreger. *Lady Gaga*. Detroit: Lucent Books, 2011.

Brill, Marlene Targ. *America in the 1980s*. Minneapolis: Twenty-First Century Books, 2010.

Gaines, Ann. *Britney Spears*. Hockessin, DE: Mitchell Lane Publishers, 2005.

Gallagher, Jim. *The Beatles*. Broomall, PA: Mason Crest Publishers, 2008.

Gnojewski, Carol. *Madonna: Express Yourself*. Berkeley Heights, NJ: Enslow Publishers, 2008.

Heos, Bridget. *Lady Gaga*. New York: Rosen Publishing Group, 2011.

Hubbard, Ben. *The History of Pop*. New York: Crabtree, 2009.

Jeffrey, Laura S. *Pink Floyd: The Rock Band*. Berkeley Heights, NJ: Enslow Publishers, 2010.

Krumenauer, Heidi. *Lady Gaga*. Hockessin, DE: Mitchell Lane Publishers, 2011.

Kuhn, Betsy. *Gay Power! The Stonewall Riots and the Gay Rights Movement, 1969*. Minneapolis: Twenty-First Century Books, 2011.

Websites

Billboard.com—Lady Gaga

http://www.billboard.com/artist/lady-gaga/1003999

Track the chart movement of Lady Gaga's latest singles on *Billboard*'s Lady Gaga page. Then head over to the main page to see which other artists are tearing up the charts.

Lady-Gaga.net

http://www.lady-gaga.net

This site is devoted to all things Gaga. Link to the latest news stories and articles on Lady Gaga, watch videos, check out a photo gallery, and much more.

Lady Gaga—Official Site

http://ladygaga.com

Lady Gaga's official site has the latest Lady Gaga news and tour dates, photos, song lyrics, and exclusive interviews with the star.

Lady Gaga Online

http://ladygagaonline.net

This fan site features tons of photos and videos, as well as a frequently updated news feed on everything Gaga.

MTV.com—Lady Gaga

http://www.mtv.com/music/artist/lady_gaga/artist.jhtml

Check out MTV's page for Lady Gaga. You'll find the latest Lady Gaga news, links to music videos and live performances, and a short biography.

INDEX

PHOTO ACKNOWLEDGMENTS

The images in this book are used with the permission of: © Charles Eshelman/FilmMagic/Getty Images, p. 1; © Sarah Lee/eyevine/ZUMA Press, p. 3; © Kevin Mazur/WireImage/Getty Images, pp. 4, 46, 67, 69, 79 (bottom), 93; AP Photo/Frank Micelotta/PictureGroup, p. 6 (left); © Jeff Kravitz/FilmMagic/Getty Images, p. 6 (right); © Dimitrios Kambouris/WireImage/Getty Images, pp. 7, 28, 38, 42, 48, 68, 79 (top), 82, 92, 94; Splash News/Newscom, pp. 8, 11, 17, 98; © Wikimedia Foundation , Inc./Beyond My Ken, p. 9; © Larry Marano/Retna Ltd., p. 12; © Larry Busacca/Getty Images, p. 13; AP Photo/Sipa Press/Patrick McMullan, p. 15; © Calvin Pia, p. 16; © Andrew Marks/Retna Ltd., p. 18; SUN/Newscom, p. 20; © Richard E. Aaron/Redferns/Getty Images, p. 22; PacificCoastNews/Newscom, p. 24; © Kevin Winter/Getty Images, pp. 26, 81; © Jason LaVeris/FilmMagic/Getty Images, p. 30; © Michael Putland/Hulton Archive/Getty Images, pp. 31, 40; © Jason Squires/WireImage/Getty Images, p. 32; © Daniel Boczarski/Redferns/Getty Images, p. 34; © Veronica S. Ibarra/FilmMagic/Getty Images, p. 36; © Dimitrios Kambouris/Getty Images, p. 37; John Grainger/Newspix/Rex USA, p. 41; ZGLR WENN photos/Newscom, p. 43; © Scott Gries/Getty Images, p. 44; © Chris Polk/FilmMagic/Getty Images, p. 49; © Bob King/Redferns/Getty Images, p. 50; © Lester Cohen/WireImage/Getty Images, p. 51 (left); © Theo Wargo/WireImage/Getty Images, p. 51 (right); John Sciulli/BEImages/Rex USA, p. 52; Margaret Norton/NBCU Photo Bank via AP Images, p. 53; © Mark Holloway/Redferns/Getty Images, p. 54; © Polk Imaging/FilmMagic/Getty Images, p. 55; Beretta/Sims/Karius/Rex USA, p. 56; Photoshot/Everett Collection, p. 57; Ella Pellegrini/Newspix/Rex USA, p. 59; Gerardo Gonzolez V./La Nacion de Costa Rica/Newscom, p. 60; © Jordan Strauss/WireImage/Getty Images, p. 61; © Bruce Glikas/FilmMagic/Getty Images, p. 62; Dana Edelson/NBCU Photo Bank via AP Images, p. 65; Everett Collection/Rex USA, p. 66; © Anwar Hussein/Getty Images, p. 70; © Dan MacMedan/USA TODAY, p. 72; © Robert Hanashiro/USA TODAY, pp. 73, 86, 89 (right); Brian J. Ritchie/Hotsauce/Rex USA, p. 74; AP Photo/PRNewsFoto/Interscope Records, p. 75; © Samir Hussein/Getty Images, p. 76 (top); © Jemal Countess/Getty Images, p. 76 (bottom); © USA TODAY, p. 77; Anthony J. Causi/Splash News/Newscom, p. 78; AP Photo/PRNewsFoto/Spirit Halloween, Seth Mayer, p. 83; AP Photo/Interscope Records, p. 87; AP Photo/Sean Kardon, p. 89 (left); Paul Drinkwater/NBC Photo Bank via AP Images, p. 90; Stephen Fernandez/Splash News/Newscom, p. 91; Smart Pictures/PacificCoastNews/Newscom, p. 97 (top left); Newspix/Rex USA, p. 97 (top right); © Ray Tamarra/Getty Images, p. 97 (bottom left); © Jon Kopaloff/Film Magic/Getty Images, p. 97 (bottom right); Ken McKay/Rex USA, p. 99.

Front cover: © Dan MacMedan/USA TODAY.

Back cover: © Kevin Mazur/WireImage/Getty Images.

Main body text set in USA TODAY Roman Regular 10.5/15.

ABOUT THE AUTHOR

Matt Doeden is a freelance author and editor. He has written hundreds of children's and young adult books, covering areas such as sports, the military, cars and motorcycles, geography and, of course, music. He and his family live in Minnesota.